THE
HEALTHY
CONVERT

Nicole Maree

THE
HEALTHY
CONVERT

Nicole Maree

hardie grant books

Published in 2017 by Hardie Grant Books, an imprint of Hardie Grant Publishing

Hardie Grant Books (Melbourne)
Building 1, 658 Church Street
Richmond, Victoria 3121
hardiegrantbooks.com.au

Hardie Grant Books (London)
5th & 6th Floors
52–54 Southwark Street
London SE1 1UN
hardiegrantbooks.co.uk

A Cataloguing-in-Publication entry is available from the catalogue of the National
Library of Australia at www.nla.gov.au
The Healthy Convert
ISBN 978 1 74379 298 8

Publisher: Pam Brewster
Managing Editor: Marg Bowman
Editor: Allison Hiew
Design Manager: Mark Campbell
Cover and text designer: Michelle Mackintosh
Photographers: Elisa Watson, Jeremy Butler
Stylist: Georgia Young
Production Manager: Todd Rechner
Production Coordinator: Rebecca Bryson
Colour reproduction by Splitting Image
Printed in China by 1010 Printing International Limited

Lovingly dedicated to Jeremy.

I thank you

for all the sacrifices you have made

for your support and guidance

for your love and laughter

for your encouragement and motivation

for being there for me always

but most of all, thank you for making me ridiculously happy.

I love you, always and forever. x

Contents.

Introduction.

Recipes are synonymous with treasured memories. Nan's cookies, Mum's 'special occasion' caramel tart and Dad's spicy fruitcake. Each warm aroma, texture and flavour hints at the love and history poured into the dish.

Family time for me has always involved cooking. The moments when we gather in one place and bring something special to the table. It's about breaking bread and sharing all our highs and lows. It's how I connect with the people I love and treasure the most.

Except for as long as I can remember, food never wanted me as a friend. I was at war with the meals I ate — battling endless stomach-aches, violent skin reactions and constant upsets. I felt completely exhausted and was turning into an emotional mess.

As I entered my twenties, I started taking back control. I went from doctor to naturopath, from dietician to nutritionist, desperate to find some answers.

I decided to start from the beginning and listen to my body. I stopped eating out and started cooking and baking as much as I could. I tried dairy free, gluten free, egg free, sugar free and raw. I learnt all I could about allergy-friendly cooking, through constant trial and error. And now I want to share this information with you.

I created these recipes to break away from the gluten-free, allergy-friendly letdowns. *The Healthy Convert* will transform your kitchen from the inside out. You'll learn to sneak vegetables into cheesecakes and fruit into delightful desserts, and how to make your own chocolatey goodness.

I'll guide you in substituting sugar, flour, eggs, oil, dairy and nuts, providing creative alternatives to your favourite sweets. You'll learn how to redefine your pantry staples and uncover the most wholesome ingredients for each dish.

I want you to love what you bake. Turn up the tunes and dance in the kitchen. Laugh and share your bench with friends and family. Create a terrible mess of batter and pastry.

With this book, I hope you'll be inspired to create your own path. Use the lessons inside these pages to enrich your lifestyle. Experiment with ingredients. Author your own recipes. Banish the social trends and ignore the dietary fads. Food is a precious gift. It's life on a plate, and it's far too delicious not to share.

Lots of love from the kitchen,

Nicole Maree

Becoming a Healthy Convert.

Let's talk about pantry essentials: sugar, flour, eggs, oil, dairy and nuts. The following chapters will discuss some must-have ingredients. These are the favourite substitutes that I use in almost all my cakes and desserts.

Every person is different, so it's important to read ingredient labels and any dietary advice carefully. Bake to your own tastes or allergies, and make adjustments that suit your lifestyle.

Ok, let's begin! Tie on a fresh apron and dive into the kitchen with a healthy curiosity. Get ready to try something tasty and brand new!

Sugar.

A spoonful might help the medicine go down — but with rising amounts hidden in our meals, refined sugar has become sickly sweet.

Sweetness doesn't have to be the enemy. If you explore beyond the processed sources, you'll uncover natural and wholesome sweeteners. The following examples are my favourite sugar alternatives, which can be picked up at your local supermarket or health food store.

Fall in love with natural sugars and find creative uses beyond the recipes in this book. Make your life sweet, golden and nutritious.

Alternative Sweeteners

Blackstrap Molasses

Best for: gingerbread, muesli cookies, oatmeal bars

How to: For 1 cup of sugar, use 1⅓ cups of blackstrap molasses. Replace no more than half the sugar in a recipe with blackstrap molasses and be careful of your flavours. You will also need to add a ½ teaspoon of bicarbonate of soda (baking soda) for each cup of molasses used.

Tips: Containing all the nutrients stripped from the sugar cane, blackstrap molasses is full of copper, iron, calcium, vitamin B6 and potassium. This dark, velvety liquid is fantastic for vegans and vegetarians.

Although it has an incredible nutritional profile, this thick syrup has an adamant flavour that can be hard on the tastebuds and also proves difficult when substituting in desserts. Blackstrap molasses works best when used in earthy recipes such as gingerbread, oatmeal bars and muesli cookies.

Brown Rice Syrup (Rice Malt Syrup)

Best for: brownies, candies, raw treats

How to: Replace 1 cup of white sugar with 1¼ cups of brown rice syrup. You will also need to reduce the liquid in the recipe by around 3 tablespoons. Brown rice syrup can be straight swapped 1:1 for liquid sugars in recipes.

Tips: Golden and thick, this toffee-flavoured syrup is created by culturing brown rice and then reducing it down to a syrup consistency. It has similar properties to golden syrup and works well as a binder in raw treats.

Brown rice syrup isn't as sweet as white sugar and refuses to 'cream' in recipes. It also comes with a pretty steep price tag. Use it in recipes when you have no maple syrup on hand and you want less sweetness in your dessert.

Coconut Nectar

Best for: raw desserts, cakes, baked treats

How to: Coconut nectar has a very thick, syrupy texture and is best straight swapped 1:1 in recipes that ask for maple syrup, corn syrup or brown rice syrup. However, you can also use ½ cup of coconut nectar to replace 1 cup of granulated sugar, but it will take some experimenting.

Tips: Coconut nectar comes from coconut palm blossoms and is a fabulous low-GI sugar alternative. This mineral-rich nectar provides a broad spectrum of amino acids and can help you feel fuller for longer. I find coconut nectar sweeter than brown rice syrup with a more toffee-caramel-like flavour.

Just like other liquid sugars, coconut nectar won't cream in recipes and can be quite expensive. However, the sticky consistency of this syrup makes it a fantastic binding ingredient for raw desserts, cakes and baked treats.

Coconut Sugar

Best for: cookies, shortbreads, bread, cakes

How to: Straight swap 1:1 for white sugar or soft brown sugar.

To make caster (superfine) sugar: Add coconut sugar to a food processor and pulse a few times until you see a fine texture.

To make powdered sugar: Put 1 cup of coconut sugar and 1 tablespoon of arrowroot starch, cornflour (cornstarch), tapioca flour or potato starch in a high-speed blender. Start with a low speed and work your way up to the highest speed. Blend until you see a powdered sugar. Transfer to a sealed glass jar and store in your pantry until needed.

Tips: Compensate for the dry texture of coconut sugar with an additional tablespoon or two of moist ingredients. Mashed sweet potato and applesauce are perfect for this. Also, keep an eye on your baked goods: the cooking time can be faster with coconut sugar.

Dried Fruit

Best for: cookies, bars, raw treats, brownies

How to: Chopped dried fruits can replace ¼ of the granulated sugar in a recipe. Puréed dried fruits can be straight swapped 1:1 with liquid sugar.

Tips: Sweet dried fruit such as dates, figs, apricots and prunes can add significant sweetness to a recipe. Dried fruit will also add fibre, binding and moisture to the recipe. Chop the dried fruit into small pieces for bursts of sweetness in your baked goods, or soak overnight in water and then purée for a liquid sugar substitute.

Unfortunately, unless it's a raw treat, you can't adequately replace all granulated sugar in a baking recipe with dried fruit.

Maple Syrup

Best for: candy, puddings, ice cream, muesli, raw treats

How to: In baking, for every 1 cup of granulated sugar, substitute ¾ cup of maple syrup. You will also need to lower the baking temperature of your oven by 4°C (25°F), add ¼ teaspoon of bicarbonate of soda (baking soda) and reduce the liquids in your recipe by 3 tablespoons. Maple syrup can be straight swapped 1:1 for other liquid sweeteners in recipes.

Tips: Buy pure, high-quality maple syrup and not the processed, high fructose corn syrup version. Pure maple syrup will cost a little more, but there's beneficial calcium, potassium, sodium and copper in each drop. Look for grade B maple syrup for a deeper and richer flavour.

Unfortunately, like all liquid sugars, maple syrup doesn't cream in a recipe the way granulated sugar does, and can cause your baked goods to brown faster. High-quality maple syrup can also be quite expensive.

Medjool Dates

Best for: brownies, piecrusts, cookies, raw treats, muesli bars

How to: Add 1 cup of pitted medjool dates and ¼ cup of water to a food processor or blender and mix until a thick purée is formed. Substitute ⅔ cup of date paste for 1 cup of regular white sugar. Make sure you remove the pits from your fresh dates before puréeing!

Tips: A bunch of medjool dates can provide a natural caramel flavour and subtle vanilla sweetness to your dessert. Full of iron, potassium, calcium, minerals and fibre, with a low GI index, medjool dates are an excellent binding agent. They can be found in the fresh produce section of your supermarket. Medjool dates are soft, gooey and sticky compared to dried dates.

Dates produce a subtle, complex flavour in baked goods. Pair them with a complementary recipe such as fruit bread, caramel treats, oatmeal bars, chocolate sweets or carrot cakes for a delicious dessert.

Puréed Fruits or Vegetables

Best for: bread, loaves, muffins, cakes

How to: Use ½ cup fruit or vegetable purée to replace 1 cup of sugar. Decrease the other liquid ingredients by 3 tablespoons.

Tips: One of my favourite ways to sweeten desserts is with fruit or vegetables. A spoonful of applesauce, squashed banana, mashed sweet potato and puréed berries are just some of the alternatives that can add natural sweetness and moisture to your baking.

Fruit can add a distinctive flavour to baked goods, so it's important to pair the ingredients well for the ultimate taste sensation. Matching mashed pineapple with carrot cake or sweet potato with chocolate cake are two great examples. I find applesauce and sweet potato provide a sugar hit without the fruity taste.

Puréed fruit or vegetables will alter the texture of your baked goods and provide an extra wet batter and moist final dessert. It takes some experimenting to get your ratios right, and you may find that your baked goods will cook faster and won't rise as high.

Rapadura Sugar

Best for: cookies, shortbreads, bread, pastries, cakes

How to: Straight swap rapadura sugar 1:1 for white sugar.

Tips: Minimally processed, high in vitamins and minerals and a fantastic substitute for white sugar, rapadura sugar has a rich, deep toffee flavour and larger crystals than regular sugar. It will also give your baked goods a rich golden colour. To retain a soft baked good, dissolve the sugar in the recipe's liquid component for approximately five minutes before adding to the remaining ingredients. Unlike coconut sugar, rapadura won't alter the texture of your dessert.

To make caster (superfine) sugar: Put rapadura sugar in a food processor and pulse a few times until you see a fine texture.

To make powdered sugar: Put 1 cup of rapadura sugar and 1 tablespoon of arrowroot starch, cornflour (cornstarch), tapioca flour or potato starch in a high-speed blender. Start with a low speed and work your way up to the highest speed. Blend until you see a powdered sugar. Transfer to a sealed glass jar and store in your pantry until you need it.

Stevia

Best for: Any recipe!

How to: Substitute 1 cup of sugar with 1 teaspoon of green leaf stevia powder. For every 1 cup of sugar substituted with stevia, add ⅛ cup of a bulking agent, such as fruit purée, apple sauce or yoghurt, to the recipe.

Tips: It's important when buying stevia that you choose green leaf stevia powder and not the white bleached powder you see in supermarkets. Supermarket stevia is often mixed with other artificial sweeteners, whereas green leaf stevia consists of the whole leaf dried at low temperatures, then ground into a fine powder. It's an all-natural sweetener that is thirty times sweeter than sugar.

As stevia is so potent, it can be hard to get the balance right when using it in recipes. The green leaf powder can also be more expensive; however, you use so little per recipe that it becomes an economical choice. It may also colour your dessert green!

White Sugar Conversion.

SWEETENER	TO REPLACE 220 g (8 oz/ 1 cup) OF WHITE SUGAR	LIQUID IN RECIPE	TIPS
Coconut sugar	140 g (5 oz/1 cup)		
Rapadura sugar	160 g (5½ oz/1 cup)		
Maple syrup	190 ml (6½ fl oz/ ¾ cup)	Reduce by 3 tablespoons	Add ¼ teaspoon of bicarbonate soda (baking soda). Lower oven temp by 4°C (25° F)
Brown rice syrup	310 ml (10½ fl oz/ 1¼ cups)	Reduce by 3 tablespoons	Add $1/16$ teaspoon of bicarbonate soda (baking soda) to recipe.
Pureed fruit or vegetables	120 g (4½ g/½ cup)	Reduce by 3 tablespoons	
Dried fruit	35 g (1¼ oz/¼ cup) approx.		Replace no more than a quarter of the sugar with dried fruit.
Medjool dates	120 g (4½ oz/⅔ cup)		Blend 1 cup of Medjool dates + ¼ cup of water until puréed.
Stevia	1 teaspoon	Add 1 tablespoon	Takes some experimenting!
Coconut nectar	125 ml (4 fl oz/½ cup)		
Blackstrap molasses	330 ml (11 fl oz/ 1⅓ cups)		Add ½ teaspoon of bicarbonate soda (baking soda) for each cup of molasses used. Replace no more than half the sugar with molasses.

Brown Sugar Conversion.

SWEETENER	TO REPLACE 200 g (7 oz/ 1 cup) BROWN SUGAR
Coconut sugar	140 g (5 oz/1 cup)
Rapadura sugar	160 g (5½ oz/1 cup)

Icing Sugar Conversion.

SWEETENER	TO REPLACE 125 g (4½ oz/1 cup) ICING (POWDERED) SUGAR	TIPS
Coconut sugar	140 g (5 oz/1 cup) coconut sugar + 1 tablespoon starch	I like to use arrowroot or cornflour as my starch.
Rapadura sugar	160 g (5½ oz/1 cup) rapadura sugar + 1 tablespoon starch	Blend in a high-speed blender or food processor until a powder forms. Store in a sealed glass jar.

Liquid Sugar Conversion.

SWEETENER	REPLACEMENTS 1:1
Maple syrup	Brown rice syrup Coconut nectar Pureed dried fruit
Honey	Brown rice syrup Maple syrup Coconut nectar Pureed dried fruit
Corn syrup	Brown rice syrup Maple syrup Coconut nectar
Golden syrup	Brown rice syrup Maple syrup Coconut nectar Molasses

Flour.

Wheat flour can be a sensitive topic. Beyond the stress it causes coeliacs, wheat substitutes can make gluten-free baking a gamble.

When cooking with alternative flours, it's important to mix and match the weights of the flours as best as possible. This helps avoid the dreaded 'gummy texture'. I'll discuss each weight type in detail, so you can perfect your signature, gluten-free blend.

Lightweight Flours (Starch)

Lightweight flours are also known as starches. These are ideal for binding ingredients and adding lightness to the final result. These starches cannot be used alone in baking and are best combined with medium- and heavyweight flours. Here are my favourites.

Arrowroot starch or tapioca flour: This easy-to-digest starch is light and fantastic for thickening and binding ingredients together. It will also add lightness and crispness to cookies.

Cornflour (cornstarch): Great for thickening sauces and adding a fluffy texture to recipes. When shopping for cornflour be on the lookout for non-GMO brands and check carefully to make sure it's gluten free. It's best used when combined with another starch and one or two mediumweight flours and an optional heavyweight flour.

Potato starch: Not to be confused with potato flour, potato starch adds lightness, moisture and lift to recipes. It's also fantastic at providing thickness and stability to vegan icing. To avoid the potato flavour, it's best used when combined with another starch and one or two mediumweight flours and an optional heavyweight flour.

Sweet rice flour: Not to be confused with white rice flour, sweet rice flour is made from short-grain glutinous rice rather than medium-grain rice. Like other starches, it's extremely efficient for thickening sauces or binding ingredients. When baking, it's best used when combined with medium- and heavyweight flours.

Mediumweight Flours

Mediumweight flours help to lighten the heavyweight flours and soften the crumb in your recipes. They can be used alone or paired with one or two lightweight flours. Here are my favourites.

Gluten-free oat flour: For coeliacs oat flour is a little risky unless you are certain your flour is 100 per cent gluten free and no cross contamination has occurred. However, if you aren't allergic to oats, oat flour can provide a great rise and flavour to your baked good. Oat flour can have a gritty texture when used alone so be sure to combine with another mediumweight flour and one or two lightweight flours to avoid this issue. To save money buy gluten-free oats and grind them in a coffee grinder or food processor to make your own oat flour.

Millet flour: If you are looking for a mildly nutty, whole-grain flavour to your baked good, millet flour is an excellent alternative. Loaded with nutrition, millet flour adds a slight yellow colour to your baking. It's best combined with another mediumweight or heavyweight flour and one or two lightweight flours.

Quinoa flour: Provides a strong earthy, bitter flavour and a protein boost to your baked goods. To remove the bitterness and create better tasting desserts, fill a clean baking tray (baking sheet) with quinoa flour and toast in the oven at 120°C (250°F) for about 25–30 minutes, stirring often. When it starts to turn golden and smell toasted, it's ready! It's best combined with another mediumweight or heavyweight flour and one or two lightweight flours.

Sorghum flour: Sorghum flour can mimic the texture of wholemeal (whole-wheat) flour, providing a very soft, light crumb and a wholesome, slightly sweet flavour to your baked good. It's one of my favourite flours and works best when combined with another mediumweight or heavyweight flour and one or two lightweight flours.

White and brown rice flour: These flours are neutral in flavour, easy to work with and provide great structure to your recipe. To avoid a gritty consistency, pulse the flour in your food processor before using to lighten the texture. White and brown rice flour are interchangeable, so use whichever suits you best. I find white rice flour is perfect for shortbreads or recipes with a crumbly texture and brown rice flour is fantastic for all other uses. They are best combined with another medium- or heavyweight flour and one or two lightweight flours.

Heavyweight Flours

Heavyweight flours give structure but don't rise much, making for a dense result. These flours are best combined with light- and mediumweight flours. Here are my favourites.

Almond flour: This has a delicious buttery flavour, and provides moisture and a nice kick of protein to your baked good. But it is quite expensive and can be difficult to use alone. It works best when used in small quantities, combined with a one or two mediumweight flours and one or two lightweight flours.

Amaranth flour: Perfect for low-rise baked goods, amaranth flour is full of nutrition and provides a distinct slightly bitter, earthy flavour and dense texture to your recipe. It's best used in combination with one or two mediumweight flours and one or two lightweight flours.

Bean flours: High in protein and fibre, bean flours are fantastic for binding and adding structure to your baked goods. They do, however, leave a very 'beany' taste, so they are better suited to savoury recipes. Combine bean flours with one or two mediumweight flours and one or two lightweight flours for the best result.

Buckwheat flour: Never fear! Despite its name, buckwheat is actually derived from a fruit and not wheat. Carrying an incredible nutritional profile and an earthy flavour, buckwheat flour will provide your recipe with a golden brown hue and a dense texture. You can buy buckwheat flour off the shelf; however, it can have a strong taste and a dark colour, making it unacceptable for desserts. I like to grind raw buckwheat kernels myself in a food processor or coffee grinder to create flour. This produces a milder-tasting and more delicate flavour for desserts. This flour is best combined with one or two mediumweight flours and one or two lightweight flours.

Coconut flour: Very tricky to use and can be hard to substitute in recipes; I find it works best for thickening sauces or batters. A tablespoon or two will quickly transform a wet batter into a thick and luscious consistency. Be careful not to add too much as coconut flour will act like a sponge, quickly slurping up any liquid in sight. It can also provide a slightly gritty, dry texture.

I find this flour only works well in small quantities (¼ cup or less) and it definitely needs to be combined with one or two heavyweight flours, one or two mediumweight flours and one or two lightweight flours.

Teff flour: A nutty, wholegrain flour that has significant binding qualities but a somewhat overpowering flavour. Use this flour in small quantities and combine with one heavyweight flour, one or two mediumweight flours and one or two lightweight flours.

Create your own gluten-free flour

GLUTEN FLOUR	GLUTEN-FREE REPLACEMENT
1 kilogram (2 lb 3 oz) flour	150 g (5½ oz) lightweight flour (use 1 or 2 kinds) + 350 g (12½ oz) mediumweight flour (use 1 or 2 kinds) + 350 g (12½ oz) heavyweight flour (use 1 or 2 kinds)
OR	
1 kilogram (2 lb 3 oz) flour	150 g (5½ oz) lightweight flour (use 1 or 2 kinds) + 700 g (1lb 9 oz) mediumweight flour (use 2 kinds)

Whisk flours together in a large bowl and store in a glass jar in the pantry or fridge.

MY GF FLOUR BLEND

This is my go-to gluten-free flour blend, which I have used in the recipes throughout this book unless I have recommended otherwise. It is a fantastic substitute for generic wheat-based plain flour and works well in cakes, cookies, slices, muffins, cupcakes, you name it!

If you are struggling to find sorghum flour, gluten-free oat flour is a great substitute. Just remember to make sure all your flours are 100 per cent gluten free if you have allergies.

Whisk the flour blend together in a large bowl and store in a glass jar.

INGREDIENTS

75 g (2¾ oz) arrowroot starch or tapioca flour

75 g (2¾ oz) potato starch

350 g (12½ oz) sorghum flour

350 g (12½ oz) brown rice flour

GLUTEN REPLACER BLEND

Add ½ teaspoon of this mix per 1 cup of gluten-free flour for bread, scrolls and doughs that rely on a gluten consistency. It can also be used as a substitute for xanthan gum or guar gum in your recipe.

Mix the ingredients together in a large bowl, store in a sealed glass jar.

INGREDIENTS

80 g (2¾ oz) ground chia seeds

80 g (2¾ oz) ground linseeds (flax seeds)

40 g (1½ oz) psyllium husk powder

Gluten-free Baking Tips

Lightness: Increase baking powder and/or bicarbonate of soda (baking soda) by 25 per cent. If the recipe asks for 1 teaspoon of baking powder, add 1¼ teaspoons instead.

Measure everything: I'm not kidding. Now is not the time to throw in a bit of this and a sprinkle of that. Use your kitchen scales to measure everything. No shortcuts!

Sift flour: Sift your flour before adding it to your other ingredients. This will lighten the dessert and provide you with tasty results.

Self-raising (self-rising) flour: Add two teaspoons of baking powder for each 150 g (5½ oz) of gluten-free plain (all-purpose) flour. Sift or whisk flour and baking powder together in a bowl before using for even distribution.

Air: Beat the batter for 2–5 minutes to create air pockets and bring lightness to the end result.

Temperature: Lower your oven temperature by 25°C (77°F), as gluten-free baking tends to brown faster and cook slower on the inside.

Baking time: Add approximately 15 minutes to the recipe time. If the recipe is for 30 minutes and you have converted it to gluten-free, you will often find it takes 45 minutes. Keep a close eye on your baking!

Binding: Most gluten-free recipes online and store-bought gluten-free baked goods will list xanthan gum or guar gum as an ingredient. These gums basically mimic the gluten response in the baked product. However, these two ingredients may cause an upset tummy for sensitive digestive systems. Instead, use the Gluten Replacer Blend listed on the page 29 to replace the xanthan or guar gum in any recipe.

Most importantly, HAVE FUN!

Eggs & Oil.

This chapter isn't to preach a fear of fat. Nor will it provide weight loss tips or ways to make your baking fat free. Oil can perform an important function, ensuring recipes stay moist and rich during the cooking process. But unnecessary added oils can be replaced with beneficial substitutes.

Eggs are considered critical in baking: they bind ingredients, prevent crumbling and encourage your dessert to rise. They're the key to making super light and fluffy spoonfuls. When substituting eggs, it's essential to take a closer look at the recipe. This will help you decide if the eggs' role is for binding or leavening.

There are a few quick ways to make this decision.

Binding

Eggs in desserts can act as a binder, holding your ingredients together while cooking to prevent crumbling.

If the recipe includes eggs plus rising ingredients, such as baking powder, bicarbonate of soda (baking soda) or baker's yeast, the eggs will help bind the ingredients together.

Leavening

Eggs can also provide air to dessert batters, allowing them to rise. If the recipe calls for no raising agents, but lists ingredients such as vinegar, citrus juice or buttermilk, then the eggs will help the recipe rise.

The fewer eggs required in a recipe, the easier it will be to substitute.

Alternatives to Eggs & Oil

Aquafaba

Best for: meringues, pavlovas, macarons, baked goods

How to: Unless the recipe says otherwise, whisk the bean water until it's frothy, then incorporate into your recipe.

1 medium egg white = 2 tablespoons of aquafaba

Tips: Aquafaba is the water in which legumes have been cooked. Yes, you heard right — it's the water that usually goes down the sink when we drain our tinned beans. When you whisk this bean juice it mimics the functional properties of egg whites, thus making a fantastic vegan substitute in meringue recipes!

Avoid the salted tinned varieties, or your recipe will taste very beany and have a strong smell! Look for chickpeas in water or white beans in water as the two main (or only) ingredients.

Beans

Best for: brownies, cakes, muffins

How to: Blend 400 g (14 oz) of salt-free tinned beans (chickpeas, white beans and black beans work best) in a high-speed blender (bean liquid and all) until a purée forms.

Bean purée can replace 75 per cent of added oil in a recipe. Replace the other 25 per cent with yoghurt for the best results.

Tips: The plant fibre found in beans will naturally improve the texture of low-fat baked goods, making them dense and fudgy. The high fibre content will also fill up your stomach and slow the rush of sugar to your bloodstream after consuming. I like to use black beans in chocolate recipes, and white beans in lighter-coloured baked goods.

Beans can make your baking denser, so for best results use them in fudgy recipes, such as brownies or mudcakes, and always use a salt-free variety to avoid a bean-scented dessert.

Bicarbonate of Soda (Baking Soda)

Best for: muffins, cakes, bread

How to: 1 egg = 2 teaspoons of bicarbonate of soda + 2 tablespoons of lemon juice or vinegar, mixed well

Tips: Bicarbonate of soda will add a fluffy and light texture to your baked good and is fantastic for leavening. However, too much bicarbonate of soda will add a bitter flavour to your recipe — so it's important to use this method when only one egg is required.

Chia Seeds/Linseeds (Flax seeds)

Best for: brownies, cakes, muffins, raw desserts, loaves

How to: 250 ml (8½ fl oz/1 cup) of oil = 190 ml (6½ fl oz/¾ cup) of water or other liquid + 4 tablespoons of chia seeds or linseeds

1 egg (binding) = 1 tablespoon of chia seeds or linseeds + 3 tablespoons of water

1 egg (leavening) = 1 tablespoon of chia seeds or linseeds + 3 tablespoons of water + ¼ teaspoon of baking powder

1 egg yolk = 1 tablespoon of chia seeds or linseeds + 2 tablespoons of water

Tips: When ground into flour or used in their whole form, chia seeds and linseeds help bind other ingredients in the recipe, preventing crumbling and dry desserts.

Whole chia seeds or linseeds can be ground in a coffee grinder or food processor if you don't have the ground variety on hand. Store ground chia seeds and linseeds in the fridge.

Cornflour (Cornstarch) or Arrowroot Starch

Best for: cookies, muffins, brownies, bread

How to: 1 egg = 1 tablespoon of starch + 2 tablespoons of water

Tips: These starches will help bind ingredients together and produce a moist, dense texture. Keep in mind they won't provide any rise to your baked good.

If more than 1 egg is required, use this in combination with another egg substitute. Always check the cornflour is gluten free and non-GMO.

Fruit or Vegetable Purée

Best for: brownies, cakes, muffins, cookies, bars

How to:

250 ml (8½ fl oz/1 cup) of oil = 180 g (6½ oz/¾ cup) of purée (approximately)

1 egg (binding or leavening) = 60 g (2 oz/¼ cup) of purée (approximately) + ½ teaspoon of baking powder

Tips: Purées can add moisture to your recipe and prevent it from drying out or crumbling. My favourite purées include unsweetened applesauce, pear, avocado, banana, pumpkin, beetroot (beet) and sweet potato. Pumpkin, sweet potato, beetroot and apple need to be cooked to purée.

Remember: the stronger the flavour of purée, the more you will be able to taste it in the final result. Be sure to match your purée to your recipe flavours.

Check your oven about 10 minutes prior to completion time, as you may find that recipes cook faster with a fruit or vegetable purée. Avoid using more than 1 cup of purée in any recipe.

Nut or Seed Butter

Best for: raw treats, unbaked goods

How to: Chilled nut or seed butters can be straight swapped 1:1 in recipes that ask for a solid fat. If your recipe asks for a liquefied fat, you can use any of the other replacements in this section.

Tips: Nut or seed butters boast an abundance of nutrients per serve and can stand in for solid fat in a recipe. Always make your own nut or seed butter at home or choose natural varieties with no added sugars, salt or trans fats. My top picks are almond, cashew nut and tahini.

Prunes or Dried Dates

Best for: brownies, chocolate cake, chocolate muffins, chocolate cookies

How to: Add 220 g (8 oz/1½ cups) of pitted prunes or pitted dates to a food processor or blender with 100 ml (3½ fl oz/⅓ cup) of water. Pulse until you achieve a puréed texture.

250 ml (8½ fl oz/1 cup) of oil = 280 g (10 oz/1 cup) of prune or date purée

Tips: Loaded with vitamins, prunes and dates provide a low-fat alternative to oil and works extremely well in chocolate baked goods. They will keep your baking soft yet crisp on the outside, just like oil!

Be aware that prune purée can sometimes produce a dry batter so you will need to add a tablespoon or two of plant-based milk or water to compensate.

Silken Tofu

Best for: brownies, cakes, muffins

How to: Replace half the oil in the recipe with tofu and the other half with fruit or vegetable purée for a healthy treat!

1 egg = 50 g (1¾ oz/¼ cup) of puréed silken tofu + ¼ teaspoon of bicarbonate of soda (baking soda)

1 egg yolk = 25 g (1 oz/⅛ cup) of puréed silken tofu

Tips: Tofu has a very mild flavour that almost disappears in baked goods while adding a protein and calcium boost to each bite.

Keep in mind that soy is a common allergen, so if you are cooking for others another substitute may suit better. Always choose organic, non-GMO soy products to avoid potential toxins.

Yoghurt

Best for: brownies, cakes, muffins, loaves

How to:

250 ml (8½ fl oz/1 cup) of oil = 185 g (6½ oz/¾ cup) of yoghurt

1 egg = 60 g (2 oz/¼ cup) of yoghurt

1 egg yolk = 30 g (1 oz/⅛ cup) of yoghurt

Tips: Yoghurt can keep cakes from tasting overly sweet and provides a dense and homemade feel. I like to use coconut yoghurt to provide richness to desserts.

If your yoghurt is overly watery try draining the yoghurt in a very fine mesh strainer before adding it to your recipes.

Zucchini (Courgettes)

Best for: cakes, loaves, muffins

How to: 250 ml (8½ fl oz/1 cup) of oil = 135 g (5 oz/1 cup) of shredded zucchini

Tips: Full of vitamin C, fibre, magnesium, vitamin A and potassium, zucchini is a fantastic alternative to oil and produces naturally moist results similar to oil in baking. Peel the zucchini and shred with a grater. Children won't even know it has been used in your baking.

Egg Conversion.

BINDING REPLACEMENT	TO REPLACE 1 EGG	TIPS
Chia seeds or Linseeds (flax seeds)	1 tablespoon + 3 tablespoons water	
Cornflour (cornstarch) or Arrowroot starch or Tapioca flour	1 tablespoon + 2 tablespoons water	
Fruit or vegetable purée	60 g (2 oz/¼ cup approx.)	Add ½ teaspoon of bicarbonate of soda (baking soda) to the recipe.
Puréed (silken or medium) tofu	50 g (1¾ oz/¼ cup)	Add ¼ teaspoon of bicarbonate of soda (baking soda) to the recipe.
Yoghurt	60 g (2 oz/¼ cup)	

Egg Conversion.

EGG WHITE REPLACEMENT	TO REPLACE 1 EGG WHITE	TIPS
Aquafaba (chickpea or bean cooking water)	2 tablespoons	Whisk mixture until frothy before use.

EGG YOLK REPLACEMENT	TO REPLACE 1 EGG YOLK
Chia seeds or linseeds (flax seeds)	1 tablespoon + 2 tablespoons of water
Silken tofu	25 g (1 oz/⅛ cup)
Yoghurt	30 g (1 oz/⅛ cup)

LEAVENING REPLACEMENT	TO REPLACE 1 EGG	TIPS
Bicarbonate of soda (baking soda)	1 teaspoon + 1 tablespoon of lemon juice or vinegar	I find apple cider vinegar or lemon juice works best.
Chia seeds linseeds (flax seeds)	1 tablespoon + 3 tablespoons of water	Add ¼ teaspoon of bicarbonate of soda (baking soda) to the recipe.
Fruit or vegetable purée	60 g (2 oz/¼ cup) approx.	Add ½ teaspoon of bicarbonate of soda (baking solda) to the recipe.

Oil Conversion.

LIQUID OIL REPLACEMENT	TO REPLACE 1 CUP
Bean purée	175 g (6 oz/¾ cup) + 60 g (2 oz/¼ cup) yoghurt
Chia seeds or linseeds (flax seeds)	4 tablespoons + 190 ml (6½ fl oz/¾ cup) water or other liquid
Fruit or vegetable purée	180 g (6½ oz/¾ cup) approx.
Prune or date purée	280 g (10 oz/1 cup) + 1–2 tablespoons liquid
Shredded zucchini (courgette)	135 g (5 oz/1 cup)
Silken tofu	100 g (3½ oz/½ cup) + 120 g (4½ oz/½ cup) fruit or vegetable purée
Yoghurt	185 g (6½ oz/¾ cup)

SOLID OIL REPLACEMENT	TO REPLACE 1 CUP
Coconut cream	250 ml (8½ fl oz/1 cup) nut or seed butter
Nut or seed butter	250 g (9 oz/1 cup)

Dairy.

Milk has long been the go-to source for creamy, rich desserts. Thick dollops of cream, smoothness in chocolate and crumbling textures in a shortcrust are all qualities produced by using dairy products. Milk is everywhere, and for anyone with an intolerance it feels difficult to avoid.

Luckily, the best alternatives are never far from reach. I'm a big fan of coconut milk, coconut cream and coconut yoghurt. With one simple ingredient, you'll be able to mimic the richness and texture of dairy.

Alternatives to Dairy

Coconut Milk

Best for: custards, fudges, sauces, pie fillings

How to: Refrigerate a tin of coconut milk overnight. After opening, you will notice the coconut cream has risen to the top and the coconut water is left on the bottom.

Use the coconut water as a straight swap 1:1 for evaporated milk. Use the solidified coconut cream as a straight swap 1:1 for cream. If you use an electric mixer and beat the solidified coconut cream it will transform into whipped cream just like its dairy alternative.

Tips: Coconut milk can provide a replacement for cream and evaporated milk in one tin! It will enhance the flavours in your recipe and provide a creamy consistency. Look for full-fat tinned coconut milk made from the meat of the coconut and with only two ingredients: coconut and water.

Coconut Yoghurt and Silken Tofu

Best for: cakes, loaves, muffins, cupcakes

How to:

250 g (9 oz/1 cup) of yoghurt = 250 g (9 oz/1 cup) of coconut yoghurt

250 g (9 oz/1 cup) of yoghurt = 200 g (7 oz/1 cup) of puréed silken tofu

Tips: Coconut yoghurt and silken tofu and vegan buttermilk (see page 48) can adequately substitute yoghurt in recipes to provide moisture and richness to the dish. If you are using yoghurt to serve with your recipe, choose coconut yoghurt for a luxurious cream alternative.

Crumbled Firm Tofu

Best for: cakes, cheesecakes, savoury dishes

How to: 250 g (9 oz/1 cup) of cottage cheese or ricotta cheese = 120 g (4½ oz/1 cup) of crumbled tofu

Tips: I find cottage cheese and ricotta cheese lack substance but come alive when you add different flavour combinations to them. Crumbled firm tofu is a great substitute when your recipe asks for cottage cheese or ricotta cheese. It provides the creaminess without adding an overpowering flavour.

Remember to always choose organic soy products free from genetic modification and unnecessary chemicals.

Plant-based Condensed Milk

Best for: decadent slices, cakes and raw treats

How to:

315 g (11 oz/1 cup) of condensed milk = 315 g (11 oz/1 cup) of soy condensed milk

315 g (11 oz/1 cup) of condensed milk = 315 g (11 oz/1 cup) of coconut condensed milk

Tips: Substitute traditional condensed milk in a straight swap 1:1 with coconut or soy condensed milk. You will hardly notice the difference in your decadent dessert!

Plant-based Ice Cream

Best for: Any dessert!

How to: Straight swap coconut or soy ice cream 1:1 for dairy ice cream.

Tips: The creamy, melt-in-your-mouth spoonful of ice cream doesn't have to be lost to you because of your intolerances. Lots of coconut and soy-based ice creams are readily available from most supermarkets and health food stores. If not, make your own!

If you don't like the taste of coconut, boycott coconut ice cream. I find that it doesn't matter which flavour you buy — there will always be a hint of coconut lingering in the background. If you make your own ice cream (recipe on page 144) it's best consumed within a day or two to avoid an icy texture.

Plant-based Milk

Best for: cakes, cookies, slices, pies, tarts

How to: Straight swap plant-based milk 1:1 for dairy milk

Tips: Plant-based milks create a soft batter or dough while retaining structure and rising properties. You can substitute milk in recipes with any plant-based milk, fruit juice or yoghurt you desire. Choose flavours you love as you may notice a small difference in taste depending on which milk you use.

I find rice, almond, coconut or soy milk best for sweet treats. Always look for milk with the smallest amount of additives or make your own at home!

Plant-based Yoghurt

Best for: cakes, muffins, bread

How to:

250 g (9 oz/1 cup) of sour cream = 250 g (9 oz/1 cup) of vegan yoghurt

250 g (9 oz/1 cup) of sour cream = 190 ml (6½ fl oz/¾ cup) of coconut milk + 1 tablespoon of vinegar or lemon juice

Tips: Plant-based yoghurt is my favourite substitute for sour cream as it provides the rich flavour and creaminess we all desire. Always use full-fat yoghurt when replacing sour cream to avoid the added thickeners and stabilisers, and always add it to a sauce after you have taken it off the heat to avoid splitting. Remember coconut yoghurt has a slight tang and a strong coconut taste compared to sour cream, so it's important to adjust your flavours accordingly.

You can also use coconut milk plus vinegar as a sour cream substitute. It works well but has a thinner consistency than traditional sour cream.

Solidified Coconut Milk

Best for: cakes, cookies, slices

How to: 250 g (9 oz/1 cup) of butter = 220 g (8 oz/1 cup of coconut cream (solidified)

Refrigerate a tin of coconut milk overnight. Once cold, the coconut cream will solidify and rise to the top, leaving the coconut water below. Straight swap the butter in your recipe 1:1 with the solidified coconut cream.

If the recipe calls for softened butter, let the cold solid coconut cream sit at room temperature before using. If the recipe asks for melted butter, melt the solid coconut cream over a low heat. If the recipe requests whipped butter, beat the solid coconut cream with a mixer or by hand.

Tips: Solidified coconut milk can be used as a fantastic flavourful replacement for butter to give a moist, light and airy texture to baked goods. The only downfall is it won't work as well for shortbreads, which rely on that real butter flavour.

Always look for full-fat tinned coconut milk made from the meat of the coconut and with only two ingredients: coconut and water. Light coconut milk contains less of the coconut flesh and often doesn't work as well for creaming or whipping.

Soy Cream Cheese

Best for: A dollop or spread here and there!

How to: Strain coconut, soy or lactose-free yoghurt overnight in the fridge by tying it up in either cheesecloth or a nut milk bag and hanging it to drain over a glass jar or bowl. This will eliminate any liquid and create a robust, creamy cheese. In the morning, discard the liquid and use your creamy mock cheese in your recipe of choice.

Straight swap strained cheese 1:1 for cream cheese.

Tips: You can buy soy-based cream cheese off the shelf, but I find it's always best to create your own to avoid the nasty additives. Strained yoghurt will provide a thick, creamy texture similar to cream cheese.

Remember that it's important to choose a yoghurt with a natural or Greek flavour for the optimal cream cheese texture. You can choose coconut yoghurt — however, it will have a strong coconut taste after straining.

Vegan Buttermilk

Best for: bread, cakes, loaves, muffins

How to: 250 ml (8½ fl oz/1 cup) of buttermilk = 250 ml (8½ fl oz/1 cup) of plant-based milk + 1 tablespoon of vinegar or lemon juice

Tips: The easiest to substitute in recipes, buttermilk can be made vegan by using plant-based milk and adding lemon juice or vinegar. It may not curdle like regular dairy-based buttermilk, but it will still serve the same purpose in a recipe. It can also be straight swapped 1:1 for yoghurt in a recipe.

For best results, allow the vinegar and milk mixture to rest for at least 10 minutes before adding to your recipe. I love using apple cider vinegar!

Dairy Conversion.

DAIRY SOURCE	TO REPLACE 220 g (8 OZ/ 1 CUP)
Buttermilk	250 ml (8½ fl oz/1 cup) plant milk + 1 tablespoon of vinegar
Sour cream	190 ml (6½ fl oz/¾ cup) coconut milk + 1 tablespoon of vinegar
	250 g (9 oz/1 cup) vegan yoghurt

Dairy Conversion.

DAIRY SOURCE	STRAIGHT SWAP 1:1
Butter	Coconut cream Coconut oil Nut, seed or coconut butter Vegan butter
Condensed milk	Coconut condensed milk Soy condensed milk
Cottage cheese/ Ricotta cheese	Crumbled tofu
Cream	Coconut cream
Cream cheese	Strained yoghurt
Evaporated milk	Coconut milk
Ice cream	Coconut ice cream Soy ice cream
Milk	Almond milk Coconut milk Macadamia nut milk Oat milk Rice milk Soy milk Other plant-based milk
Yoghurt	Coconut yoghurt Silken tofu Vegan buttermilk

Nuts.

So many classic desserts demand a crunch factor. It's the perfect marriage of sweet and gooey, with a surprising explosion of crunch. Nuts are a fantastic source of texture, and you can butter them, candy them, roast and toast them.

Before we begin, identify the difference between personal taste and nut allergy. If you don't like the taste of certain nuts, explore the alternatives listed in this chapter. If you're subject to anaphylactic shock, don't experiment or push the boundaries. Stick to what you know and always be sure to check ingredient lists for any triggers.

Nut Conversion.

NUT SOURCE	STRAIGHT SWAPS 1:1
Almonds	Crushed gluten-free biscuits Gluten-free oats Hazelnuts Peanuts Sunflower kernels
Cashew nuts	Fresh coconut meat Macadamia nuts Shredded coconut
Hazelnuts	Almonds Buckwheat kernels Sunflower kernels
Macadamia nuts	Cashew nuts Pepitas (pumpkin seeds) Shredded coconut Sunflower kernels
Nut butter	Coconut butter Seed butter
Peanuts	Almonds Buckwheat kernels Crushed gluten-free biscuits Sunflower kernels
Pecans	Crushed gluten-free biscuits Gluten-free oats Sunflower kernels Walnuts
Pine nuts	Pepitas (pumpkin seeds) Sesame seeds Shredded coconut Sunflower kernels
Walnuts	Crushed gluten-free biscuits Gluten-free oats Pecans Sunflower kernels

53

TINY
TREATS

RUMMY RAISIN TREATS

DAIRY FREE, GLUTEN FREE, VEGAN

Blend 100 g (3½ oz) of the desiccated coconut with all the remaining ingredients except the raisins in a food processor until the mixture is combined and starts to stick together. Transfer to a large bowl and fold in the raisins.

Take a tablespoon of the mixture, form it into a ball and roll it in the remaining coconut. Repeat with the remaining mixture.

Transfer the treats to an airtight container and refrigerate for 1 hour to set.

They can last in an airtight container in the fridge for up to 1 week or in the freezer for up to 2 months.

Makes 22 treats.

140 g (5 oz) unsweetened desiccated coconut

140 g (5 oz) medjool dates, pitted

200 g (7 oz) dry-roasted unsalted cashew nuts

20 g (¾ oz) coconut oil, softened

30 g (1 oz/¼ cup) cacao powder

25 ml (¾ fl oz) sweet rum

50 g (1¾ oz) raisins

NOTE
For a nut-free variation, you can replace the cashew nuts with gluten-free arrowroot biscuits.

TAHINI TREATS

DAIRY FREE, GLUTEN FREE, NUT FREE, VEGAN

I adore these snacks and keep them on standby in the freezer. They're perfect for those late-night sweet cravings or a mid-morning energy boost.

Blend 80 g (2¾ oz) of the desiccated coconut with all the remaining ingredients in a food processor until the mixture is combined and starts to stick together.

Transfer to a large bowl and freeze for 30 minutes to firm up.

Take a heaped tablespoon of the mixture, form it into a ball and roll it in the remaining coconut. Repeat with the remaining mixture.

Transfer the treats to an airtight container and freeze for 15 minutes to set.

They can last in an airtight container in the fridge for up to 1 week or in the freezer for 2 months.

Makes 20 treats.

110 g (4 oz) unsweetened desiccated coconut

220 g (8 oz) hulled tahini

80 ml (2½ fl oz/⅓ cup) maple syrup

80 g (2¾ oz) currants

50 g (1¾ oz/⅓ cup) sesame seeds

80 g (2¾ oz) dried dates, finely chopped

80 g (2¾ oz) dried apricots, diced

COOKIE DOUGH TREATS

DAIRY FREE, GLUTEN FREE, NUT FREE, VEGAN

Preheat the oven to 180°C (160°C fan forced/350°F). Line a large 38 cm × 25 cm (15 in × 10 in) baking tray (baking sheet) with baking paper.

Mix the chia seeds with 30 ml (1 fl oz) water. Set aside to become gelatinous.

Add the coconut cream, coconut sugar, sea salt, vanilla extract, flour, bicarbonate of soda and chia mixture to a large bowl. Mix until a dough forms. Fold in half the chocolate.

Take a heaped tablespoon of the mixture, roll it into a ball and place it on the prepared baking tray. Repeat with the remaining mixture. Stud the balls with the remaining chocolate.

Bake in the oven for 15–20 minutes, or until lightly golden. Allow the treats to cool. Serve with ice cream, or on their own.

Store them in an airtight container in the pantry or fridge for up to 1 week.

Makes 24 treats

25 g (1 oz) chia seeds

175 ml (6 fl oz) tinned coconut cream

125 g (4½ oz) coconut sugar

1½ teaspoons ground sea salt

2 teaspoons vanilla extract

310 g (11 oz) gluten-free plain (all-purpose) flour

1 teaspoon bicarbonate of soda (baking soda)

60 g (2 oz) vegan milk chocolate, roughly chopped

STRAWBERRY SHORTCAKE BALLS

DAIRY FREE, GLUTEN FREE, VEGAN

In a food processor, blend the freeze-dried strawberries to a breadcrumb-like texture. Transfer to a large bowl.

In a small saucepan over a low heat, add cacao butter, cashew nut butter and coconut butter. Stir until melted.

Add all the remaining ingredients to the freeze-dried strawberries. Add the melted cacao-butter mixture and stir until thoroughly combined.

Refrigerate the mixture for 30 minutes. Once it's set, take a heaped tablespoon of the mixture and roll it into a ball. Repeat with the remaining mixture.

Transfer the balls to an airtight container and refrigerate for 1 hour to set.

They can last in an airtight container in the fridge for up to 1 week.

Makes 22 balls

30 g (1 oz) freeze-dried strawberries

80 g (2¾ oz) raw cacao butter

70 g (2½ oz) cashew nut butter

150 g (5½ oz) coconut butter

200 g (7 oz) gluten-free vegan arrowroot biscuits, crushed

30 g (1 oz) unsweetened desiccated coconut

40 ml (1½ fl oz) rice malt syrup

1 teaspoon vanilla extract

NOTE
You can substitute the raw cacao butter for vegan white chocolate or extra coconut butter.

LEMON & TURMERIC BALLS

DAIRY FREE, GLUTEN FREE, NUT FREE, VEGAN

Blend 140 g (5 oz) of the sunflower kernels with all the remaining ingredients in a food processor until the mixture is combined and starts to stick together.

Freeze the mixture for 15 minutes or until firm. Finely chop the remaining sunflower kernels.

Once the mixture is firm, take a tablespoon of the mixture, form it into a ball and roll it in the chopped sunflower kernels. Repeat with the remaining mixture.

Transfer the treats to an airtight container and freeze for 1 hour to set.

They can last in the freezer in an airtight container for up to 2 months.

Makes 22 balls

220 g (8 oz) raw sunflower kernels

60 ml (2 fl oz/¼ cup) rice malt syrup

150 g (5½ oz) medjool dates, pitted

55 g (2 oz) unsweetened desiccated coconut

80 g (2¾ oz) dried apricots, roughly chopped

2 teaspoons chia seeds

1 teaspoon finely grated lemon zest

30 ml (1 fl oz) freshly squeezed lemon juice

1 teaspoon vanilla extract

½ teaspoon ground ginger

½ teaspoon ground turmeric

20 g (¾ oz) coconut oil, softened

65

CHOC-COCO ROUGHIES

DAIRY FREE, GLUTEN FREE, VEGAN

Line a large 38 cm × 25 cm (15 in × 10 in) baking tray with baking paper.

In a medium saucepan over a low heat, combine the cashew nut butter, rice malt syrup and coconut oil until melted and combined.

Remove from the heat and stir in the carob powder, vanilla and melted chocolate. Add the coconut and mix well.

Using a tablespoon, spoon dollops of the mixture onto the prepared tray.

Put the tray in the freezer for 30 minutes to set.

Store in an airtight container in the freezer for up to 2 months.

Makes 30 Choc-coco roughies

150 g (5½ oz) cashew nut butter

100 ml (3½ fl oz) rice malt syrup

50 g (1¾ oz) coconut oil

35 g (1¼ oz) carob powder

2 teaspoons vanilla extract

50 g (1¾ oz) vegan milk chocolate, melted

200 g (7 oz) unsweetened desiccated coconut

NOTES

You can replace the cashew nut butter with any nut or seed butter, and the carob powder with cacao powder.

Use these for topping your favourite smoothies or ice cream!

MINT-AS FUDGE

DAIRY FREE, GLUTEN FREE, NUT FREE, VEGAN

Line the base and sides of a 17 cm × 17 cm (6¾ in × 6¾ in) square cake tin with baking paper, ensuring the paper hangs over the sides of the tin for easy removal.

For the chocolate swirl, heat the condensed milk, sugar, maple syrup and coconut butter in a saucepan over a medium–low heat. Cook, stirring, without boiling for 5 minutes or until the sugar has dissolved.

For the mint swirl, heat the condensed milk, maple syrup and coconut butter in a saucepan over a medium–low heat. Cook, stirring, without boiling until all the ingredients are melted.

Remove each saucepan from the heat. To the first saucepan add the milk chocolate and mix well, until the chocolate is melted. To the second saucepan add the cacao butter, peppermint extract and spirulina (for colour) and mix well until combined.

Working quickly, spoon dollops of both mixtures into the prepared tin, alternating between the two colours. Using a skewer, swirl the two together to create a marble effect. Put in the freezer for 2 hours to set.

Remove from the tin, discard the baking paper and slice into 30 pieces.

Store the fudge in an airtight container in the freezer for up to 1 month.

Makes 30 pieces

CHOCOLATE SWIRL

80 g (2¾ oz/¼ cup) coconut condensed milk

35 g (1¼ oz) coconut sugar

35 ml (1¼ fl oz) maple syrup

75 g (2¾ oz) coconut butter

70 g (2½ oz) vegan milk chocolate, roughly chopped

MINT SWIRL

115 g (4 oz/½ cup) coconut condensed milk

35 ml (1¼ fl oz) maple syrup

75 g (2¾ oz) coconut butter

70 g (2½ oz) vegan raw cacao butter

1 teaspoon peppermint extract

½ teaspoon spirulina powder

NOTE
You can use vegan white chocolate in place of cacao butter.

NEAPOLITAN FUDGE

DAIRY FREE, GLUTEN FREE, NUT FREE, VEGAN

This is for my siblings, Katanya and John. In our house there were never any arguments about Neapolitan ice cream. Kat would steal the strawberry, and John would scoop from the chocolate. Me? I'd always try to take from all three!

Line the base and sides of a 10.5 cm × 20 cm (4¼ in × 8 in) loaf (bar) tin with baking paper.

For the chocolate layer, put the condensed milk, sugar, maple syrup and coconut butter in a saucepan over a medium–low heat. Cook, stirring, without boiling for 5 minutes or until the sugar has dissolved. Remove from the heat and add the vegan milk chocolate. Mix well until the chocolate is melted. Working quickly, spoon into the prepared loaf tin and smooth the top. Put in the freezer for 30 minutes.

For the strawberry layer, purée the strawberries in a blender. Strain the purée through a fine-mesh sieve, reserving the liquid. Discard the pulp and put the liquid, condensed milk, sugar, maple syrup and coconut butter in a saucepan over a medium–low heat. Cook, stirring, without boiling for 5 minutes or until the sugar has dissolved. Remove from the heat and add the white chocolate. Mix well until the chocolate is melted. Working quickly, evenly spoon the mixture on top of the chocolate layer, smoothing the top. Freeze for 30 minutes.

For the vanilla layer, stir the condensed milk and coconut butter in a saucepan over a medium–low heat without boiling until melted. Remove from the heat and add the white chocolate and vanilla extract. Mix well until the chocolate is melted. Working quickly, evenly spoon the mixture on top of the strawberry layer, smoothing the top. Put in the freezer for 2 hours to set.

Remove from the tin and discard the baking paper. Cut the fudge into 12 squares.

Store the fudge in an airtight container in the freezer for up to 1 month.

Makes 12 squares

CHOCOLATE LAYER

55 g (2 oz) coconut condensed milk

25 g (1 oz) coconut sugar

25 ml (¾ fl oz) maple syrup

50 g (1¾ oz) coconut butter

50 g (1¾ oz) vegan milk chocolate, roughly chopped

STRAWBERRY LAYER

100 g (3½ oz) fresh strawberries, hulled

55 g (2 oz) coconut condensed milk

25 g (1 oz) coconut sugar

2 teaspoons maple syrup

50 g (1¾ oz) coconut butter

60 g (2 oz) vegan white chocolate, roughly chopped

VANILLA LAYER

105 g (3½ oz/⅓ cup) coconut condensed milk

60 g (2 oz) coconut butter

50 g (1¾ oz) vegan white chocolate, roughly chopped

1 teaspoon vanilla extract

NOTE

If you can't find vegan white chocolate you can also use raw cacao butter buttons.

PEANUT BERRYBUTTER FUDGE

DAIRY FREE, GLUTEN FREE, VEGAN

Line the base and sides of a 10.5 cm × 20 cm (4¼ in × 8 in) loaf (bar) tin with baking paper, ensuring the paper hangs over the sides of the tin for easy removal.

For the peanut layer, put the condensed milk, sugar, maple syrup, peanut butter and coconut butter in a saucepan over a medium–low heat. Cook, stirring, without boiling for 5 minutes or until the sugar has dissolved. Remove from the heat and add the vegan white chocolate, mixing well until the chocolate is melted. Working quickly, spoon the mixture into the prepared loaf tin and smooth the top. Put in the freezer for 30 minutes.

For the berry layer, purée the raspberries in a high-speed blender. Strain the purée through a fine-mesh sieve, reserving the liquid. Discard (or save for later and eat) the pulp and put the liquid, condensed milk and coconut butter in a saucepan over a medium–low heat.

Cook, stirring, without boiling until the coconut butter has melted. Remove from the heat and add the white chocolate, mixing well until the chocolate is melted. Working quickly, evenly spoon the mixture into the prepared tin and spread on top of the peanut layer, smoothing the top. Put in the freezer for 2 hours.

Remove from the tin and discard the baking paper. Cut the fudge into 12 slices.

Store in an airtight container in the freezer for up to 1 month.

Makes 12 slices

PEANUT LAYER

80 g (2¾ oz/¼ cup) coconut condensed milk

35 g (1¼ oz) coconut sugar

35 ml (1¼ fl oz) maple syrup

50 g (1¾ oz) peanut butter

55 g (2 oz) coconut butter

70 g (2½ oz) vegan white chocolate, roughly chopped

BERRY LAYER

100 g (3½ oz) fresh raspberries

80 g (2¾ oz/¼ cup) coconut condensed milk

100 g (3½ oz) coconut butter

120 g (4½ oz) vegan white chocolate, roughly chopped

NOTES

You can replace the peanut butter with tahini, sunflower kernel butter or any nut or seed butter of choice!

You can replace the coconut sugar with rapadura sugar and the maple syrup with rice malt syrup.

You can replace the vegan white chocolate with raw cacao butter buttons.

JERSEY CARAMELS

DAIRY FREE, GLUTEN FREE, VEGAN

This one's for Mum. When we were growing up, jersey caramels were our favourite movie treat. We'd always finish the bag before the credits rolled.

Line the base and sides of a 17 cm × 17 cm (6¾ in × 6¾ in) square cake tin with baking paper, ensuring the paper hangs over the sides of the tin for easy removal.

For the first caramel layer, put half the condensed milk, half the sugar, half the maple syrup and half the cashew nut butter in a saucepan over a medium–low heat.

Cook, stirring, without boiling for 5 minutes or until the sugar has dissolved. Remove from the heat and add half the vegan white chocolate and mix well, ensuring the chocolate is melted. Working quickly, spoon the mixture into the prepared tin and smooth the top. Put in the freezer for 30 minutes.

For the cream layer, melt the coconut butter, cashew nut butter and maple syrup in a saucepan over a medium–low heat until it's smooth and combined. Remove from the heat and add the vanilla extract. Evenly spread the cream on top of the caramel layer, smoothing the top, and put it in the freezer to set for 1 hour. This layer needs to be completely set before adding the top caramel layer.

For the last caramel layer, heat the remaining condensed milk, sugar, maple syrup and cashew nut butter in a saucepan over a medium–low heat. Cook, stirring, without boiling for 5 minutes or until the sugar has dissolved.

Remove from the heat and add the remaining vegan white chocolate, mixing well and ensuring the chocolate is melted. Working quickly, spread the mixture evenly on top of the cream layer, smoothing the top. Return the tin to the freezer for 2 hours.

Slice into small cubes.

Store in an airtight container in the freezer for up to 1 month.

Makes 48 caramels

CARAMEL LAYERS

160 g (5½ oz/½ cup) coconut condensed milk

70 g (2½ oz) coconut sugar

70 ml (2¼ fl oz) maple syrup

150 g (5½ oz) cashew nut butter

140 g (5 oz) vegan white chocolate, roughly chopped

CREAM LAYER

100 g (3½ oz) coconut butter

70 g (2½ oz) cashew nut butter

30 ml (1 fl oz) maple syrup

½ teaspoon vanilla extract

SLICES
AND BARS

TRIPLE LAYER CARAMEL CREAM

DAIRY FREE, GLUTEN FREE, VEGAN

Line the base and sides of a 17 cm × 17 cm (6¾ in × 6¾ in) square cake tin with baking paper, ensuring paper hangs over the sides of the tin for easy removal.

Combine all the base ingredients in a food processor until a dough has formed. Press evenly into the prepared cake tin, and freeze while you prepare the remaining layers.

For the cream layer, put the cashew nuts in a bowl and cover with boiling water. Set aside to soak for 30 minutes. Drain and rinse very well.

Blend the drained cashew nuts in a food processor or high-speed blender with coconut, vanilla, milk, coconut oil and rice malt syrup until smooth and creamy. Spread over the base layer and freeze for 30 minutes.

For the caramel layer, carefully blend the dates, salt and water in a food processor until smooth.

Spread the caramel layer onto the cream layer. Freeze for 1 hour.

Remove from the tin, cut into slices and serve.

Store the remaining slices in an airtight container in the fridge for up to 1 week or in the freezer for up to 1 month.

Makes 18 slices

BASE

60 g (2 oz/½ cup) cacao powder

90 ml (3 fl oz) rice malt syrup

200 g (7 oz) raw walnuts

CREAM LAYER

230 g (8 oz) dry-roasted unsalted cashew nuts

50 g (1¾ oz) unsweetened desiccated coconut

½ teaspoon vanilla extract

80 ml (2½ fl oz/⅓ cup) plant-based milk

45 g (1½ fl oz) coconut oil

70 ml (2¼ fl oz) rice malt syrup

CARAMEL LAYER

260 g (9 oz) soft medjool dates, pitted

¼ teaspoon ground sea salt

40 ml (1¼ fl oz) boiling water

CHRISTMAS PUDDING SLICE

DAIRY FREE, GLUTEN FREE, VEGAN

All the goodness of Christmas pudding, jam-packed into a hedgehog slice – rum included.

In a small bowl mix the raisins and rum to combine and leave to soak for 30 minutes.

Line the base and sides of a 17 cm × 17 cm (6¾ in × 6¾ in) cake tin with baking paper, ensuring the paper hangs over the sides of the tin for easy removal.

In a food processor pulse the arrowroot biscuits until slightly crushed. Transfer to a large bowl.

Add the coconut, cacao powder, apricots, cranberries, orange zest and soaked raisins. Mix to combine.

In a saucepan over a medium–low heat, mix the almond butter, rice malt syrup and coconut oil until melted and smooth. Remove from the heat and add to the dry ingredients. Mix well.

Press the mixture into the prepared cake tin. Freeze for 1 hour or until firm.

Remove from the tin, slice into squares and serve.

Store the remaining slices in an airtight container in the freezer for up to 1 month.

Makes 16 slices

100 g (3½ oz) raisins

50 ml (1¾ fl oz) sweet rum

200 g (7 oz) gluten-free, vegan arrowroot biscuits

40 g (1½ oz) unsweetened desiccated coconut

40 g (1½ oz/⅓ cup) cacao powder

100 g (3½ oz) dried apricots, roughly chopped

100 g (3½ oz) dried cranberries

1 tablespoon finely grated orange zest

135 g (4¾ oz) almond butter

90 ml (3 fl oz) rice malt syrup

40 g (1½ oz) coconut oil

81

NOTE
You can replace the almond butter with a seed butter of choice to make this recipe nut free.

GINGER BARS
DAIRY FREE, GLUTEN FREE, VEGAN

Preheat the oven to 180°C (160°C fan forced/350°F).

Line the base and sides of a 26 cm × 16.5 cm (10¼ in × 6½ in) slice tin with baking paper, allowing the sides to overhang.

Pulse the brown rice flour and sunflower kernels in a food processor until finely milled. Transfer to a large bowl. Add the coconut sugar, desiccated coconut and ground ginger. Mix well.

In a separate bowl, mix the rice malt syrup, coconut cream, coconut oil, bicarbonate of soda and milk.

Add the wet mixture to the dry. Stir to combine. Evenly press the mixture into the prepared slice tin.

Bake for 20 minutes or until golden brown. The slice will still feel a little soft but will firm up as it cools. Cool completely in the tin.

For the topping, blend the medjool dates in a small food processor or high-speed blender until a purée forms. Set aside.

Melt the almond butter, white chocolate and maple syrup in a saucepan over a low heat until thick and melted. Once combined, remove from the heat and add the vanilla extract, ginger and date purée. Mix well.

Spread the mixture over the cooled base and smooth the top. Sprinkle with crystalised ginger.

Refrigerate the slice for 2 hours. Remove from the tin, cut into bars and serve.

Store the remaining bars in an airtight container in the fridge for up to 1 week.

Makes 12 bars

BASE

180 g (6½ oz) brown rice flour

140 g (5 oz) sunflower kernels

90 g (3 oz) coconut sugar

60 g (2 oz) desiccated coconut

1 teaspoon ground ginger (see notes)

45 ml (1½ fl oz) rice malt syrup

70 g (2½ oz) tinned coconut cream

70 g (2½ oz) coconut oil, melted

½ teaspoon bicarbonate of soda (baking soda)

30 ml (1 fl oz) plant-based milk

TOPPING

150 g (5½ oz) medjool dates, pitted

25 g (1 oz) almond butter

100 g (3½ oz) vegan white chocolate, coarsely chopped

70 ml (2¼ fl oz) maple syrup

½ teaspoon vanilla extract

3 teaspoons ground ginger

100 g (3½ oz) crystalised ginger, finely diced

NOTES

Always taste the mixture as you go and add more ground ginger if needed. Powdered ginger can vary in strength depending on how old or fresh it is.

You can substitute tahini or sunflower kernel butter for the almond butter to make this recipe nut free.

PEPPERMINT SLICE

DAIRY FREE, GLUTEN FREE, VEGAN

Forget after-dinner mints. This cheesecake is every bit as creamy and refreshing. A welcome treat after any meal.

Put the cashew nuts in a large bowl and cover with boiling water. Soak for 30 minutes.

Line the base and sides of a 20 cm × 20 cm × 7 cm deep (8 in × 8 in × 2¾ in) square springform cake tin with baking paper.

Blend the base ingredients and 30 ml (1 fl oz) water in a food processor until the mixture starts to come together. Press the mixture firmly into the base of the prepared tin. Put it in the freezer while you prepare the filling.

Drain and rinse the cashew nuts very well. Blend the drained cashew nuts, rice malt syrup, coconut oil, coconut cream, mint leaves and lemon juice in your food processor until smooth and well combined. Add the peppermint extract and spirulina and blend to combine. Pour the mixture over the base and freeze for 3 hours to set.

To serve, remove from the freezer and sit at room temperature for 30 minutes. Using a warm, sharp knife, cut the cheesecake into 18 slices.

For the topping, in a bowl mix the rice malt syrup, coconut oil, cacao powder and vanilla extract until smooth. Using a piping (icing) bag or spoon, drizzle the chocolate over the squares.

Store the remaining slices in an airtight container in the freezer for up to 1 month.

Makes 18 slices

BASE

70 g (2½ oz) medjool dates, pitted

40 ml (1¼ fl oz) rice malt syrup

30 g (1 oz) unsweetened desiccated coconut

300 g (10½ oz) raw almonds

25 g (1 oz) cacao powder

FILLING

300 g (10½ oz) raw cashew nuts

180 ml (6 fl oz) rice malt syrup

60 g (2 oz) coconut oil

400 ml (13½ fl oz) tinned coconut cream

5 g (¼ oz/¼ cup) fresh mint leaves

60 ml (2 fl oz/¼ cup) lemon juice

2 teaspoons peppermint extract

¼ teaspoon spirulina

TOPPING

35 ml (1¼ fl oz) rice malt syrup

35 g (1¼ oz) coconut oil, melted

25 g (1 oz) cacao powder

1 teaspoon vanilla extract

NOTE
You can use maple syrup in place of rice malt syrup.

CRISPY RICE BARS

DAIRY FREE, GLUTEN FREE, NUT FREE, VEGAN

Line the base and sides of a 17 cm × 17 cm (6¾ in × 6¾ in) square cake tin with baking paper, ensuring the paper hangs over the sides of the tin for easy removal.

Combine the tahini and rice malt syrup in a small saucepan over a medium heat until smooth and creamy. Remove from the heat and stir in the vanilla extract and sea salt.

Divide the cereal equally between two large mixing bowls. Divide the desiccated coconut evenly between each bowl. Add the cacao powder to one bowl and mix well.

Divide the tahini mixture evenly between both bowls. Mix both bowls until the cereal is well coated.

Evenly spread the white mixture into half of the prepared tin and the chocolate into the other half.

Place a piece of baking paper over the top of the cereal to keep your hands from getting sticky, then press down firmly to pack the cereal tightly into the bottom of the pan. The harder you press, the better.

Put the cake tin in the freezer to cool for 45 minutes. Remove the tin from the freezer and drizzle the white bars with the white chocolate and the chocolate bars with the milk chocolate.

Slice and serve!

Store any leftover bars in an airtight container in your fridge for up to a week.

Makes 16

130 g (4½ oz) hulled tahini

190 ml (6½ fl oz) rice malt syrup

1 teaspoon vanilla extract

¼ teaspoon ground sea salt

100 g (3½ oz) gluten-free rice crisp cereal (see notes)

60 g (2 oz) unsweetened desiccated coconut

30 g (1 oz/¼ cup) cacao powder

50 g (1¾ oz) vegan white chocolate, melted

50 g (1¾ oz) vegan milk chocolate, melted

NOTES

You can substitute nut or seed butter of your choice for the tahini.

Be sure to use rice crisp cereal not rice puffs for an ultra crunchy treat.

CHOCOLATE BROWNIES

DAIRY FREE, GLUTEN FREE, VEGAN

Preheat the oven to 180°C (160°C fan forced/350°F). Line the base and sides of a 26 cm × 16.5 cm (10¼ in × 6½ in) slice tin with baking paper, allowing the sides to overhang.

Drain the chickpeas, reserving 60 ml (2 fl oz/¼ cup) of chickpea water (aquafaba) in a bowl. Transfer the chickpeas to a container in the fridge and keep for another use.

In a small bowl thoroughly mix the chia seeds and 85 ml (2¾ fl oz) water. Set aside to become gelatinous.

In a large bowl, mix the aquafaba, chia mixture, cacao powder, stevia, baking powder, coffee, salt and vanilla until combined.

Put the coconut oil, sugar and applesauce in a saucepan over a medium heat. Cook, constantly stirring until melted and ingredients are barely bubbling.

Add the hot coconut oil mixture to the chocolate mixture and stir until well combined.

Add the flour and mix to form a thick batter. The mixture will remain slightly lumpy. Allow the batter to rest for 20 minutes.

After resting, gently stir in the chocolate and pour the mixture into the prepared tin. Use a spatula to smooth the batter evenly into the corners of the pan.

Bake for 30 minutes. A toothpick inserted into the centre should reveal very moist crumbs. Allow to cool completely in the pan on a wire rack before removing.

Slice and garnish the brownies with a sprinkling of chopped hazelnuts.

Store any leftover brownies in an airtight container in the fridge for up to a week.

Makes 12 large brownies

400 g (14 oz) tin salt-free chickpeas

25 g (1 oz) chia seeds

100 g (3½ oz) cacao powder

1 teaspoon green leaf stevia

1 teaspoon baking powder

½ teaspoon finely ground coffee

1 teaspoon ground sea salt

20 ml (¾ fl oz) vanilla extract

100 g (3½ oz) coconut oil

180 g (6½ oz) rapadura sugar

125 g (4½ oz) unsweetened applesauce

180 g (6½ oz) gluten-free plain (all-purpose) flour

125 g (4½ oz) vegan milk chocolate, roughly chopped

dry-roasted unsalted hazelnuts, roughly chopped, to garnish

DATE CRUMBLE SLICE

DAIRY FREE, GLUTEN FREE, VEGAN

Preheat oven to 180°C (160°C fan forced/350°F). Line the base and sides of a 17 cm × 17 cm (6¾ in × 6¾ in) square cake tin with baking paper, ensuring the paper hangs over the sides of the tin for easy removal.

Combine the dates, maple syrup and 120 ml (4 fl oz) of water in a medium saucepan over a medium–high heat. Bring to the boil, stirring frequently, for about 3 minutes or until the dates are pulpy. Remove from heat, stir in the orange juice and set aside to cool.

Pulse the walnuts in a food processor until a flour forms. Set aside in a large bowl.

Blend the coconut milk, vanilla and sugar in a food processor until combined. Add the flour, sea salt, cinnamon, bicarbonate of soda and walnut flour. Process until a dough forms, being careful not to overmix.

Evenly press three-quarters of the dough into the base of the prepared pan. Spread the date mixture over the top.

Crumble the remaining dough mixture over the date mixture so the dates are completely covered, pressing the dough gently into the date mixture with your fingertips.

Bake for 30–35 minutes, or until golden. Allow to cool completely in the tin.

Remove from the tin and slice.

Store in an airtight container in the fridge for up to a week.

Makes 6 large slices or 12 small slices

320 g (11 ½ oz) dried dates, pitted and roughly chopped

50 ml (1¾ fl oz) maple syrup

80 ml (2½ fl oz/⅓ cup) freshly squeezed orange juice

165 g (6 oz) raw walnuts

145 ml (5 fl oz) tinned coconut milk

1 teaspoon vanilla extract

80 g (2¾ oz) coconut sugar

345 g (12 oz) gluten-free plain (all-purpose) flour

¼ teaspoon ground sea salt

1 teaspoon ground cinnamon

½ teaspoon bicarbonate of soda (baking soda)

NOTE
You can replace the walnuts with gluten-free oats to make this recipe nut free.

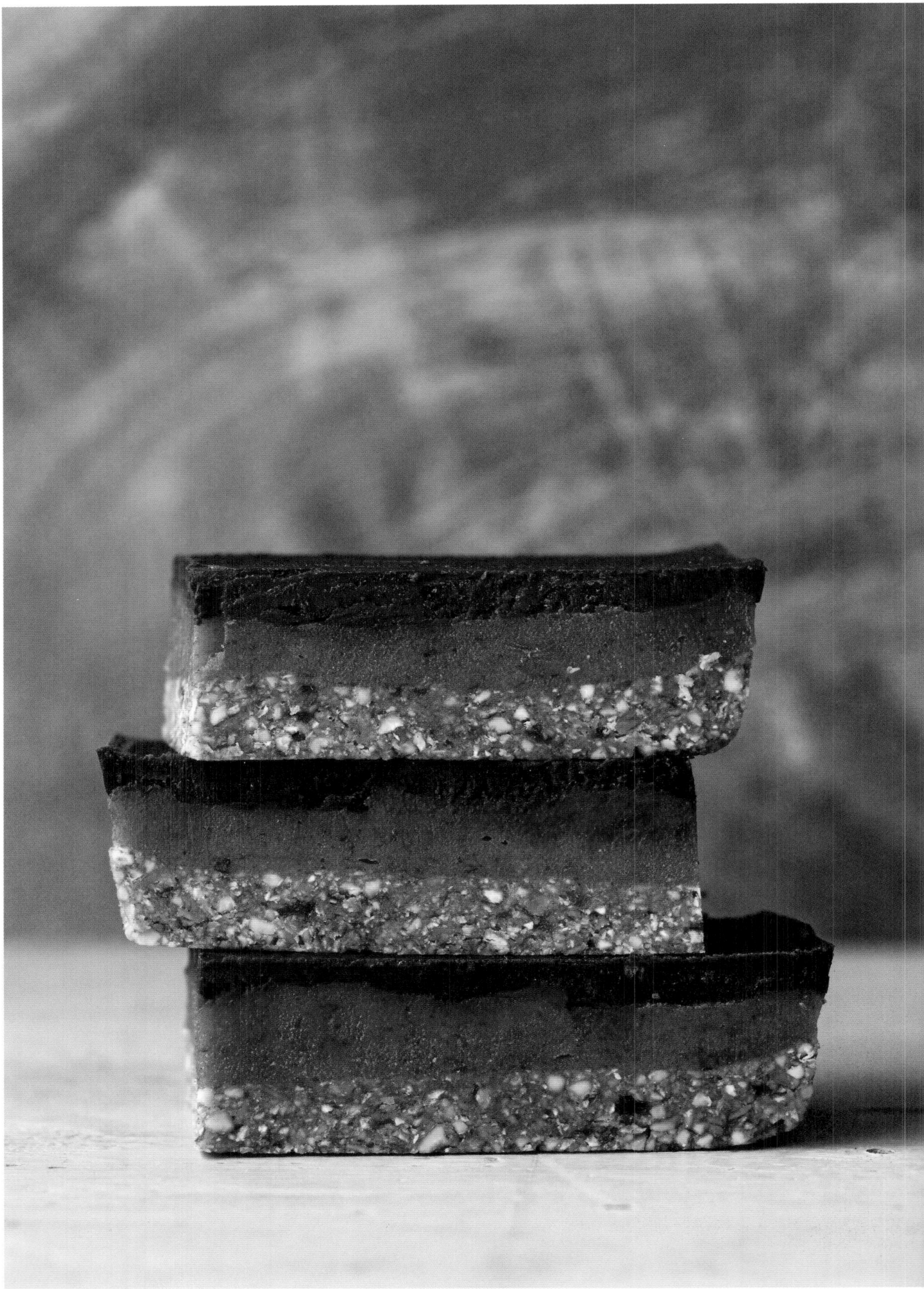

CHOC CARAMEL SLICE

DAIRY FREE, GLUTEN FREE, VEGAN

Oozy, gooey and full of sticky goodness, this slice is for the fussy eaters who criticise allergy-friendly treats. Prepare to be converted.

Line the base and sides of a 17 cm × 17 cm (6¾ in × 6¾ in) square cake tin with baking paper, ensuring the paper hangs over the sides of the tin for easy removal.

Blend all the base ingredients and 30 ml (1 fl oz) water in a food processor until a dough is formed and the mixture sticks together when pressed. Add more water if the mixture is too dry.

Using a wet spoon, press the base mixture evenly into the prepared tin and freeze for 30 minutes.

Blend all the caramel ingredients in a high-speed blender or food processor until smooth. The mixture will look a little split. Transfer to a small saucepan over a medium–low heat and cook until the mixture comes together and forms a smooth, thick caramel. Spread the caramel on top of the base. Freeze for 30 minutes.

Mix all the chocolate ingredients in a bowl until smooth. Spread on top of the caramel. Freeze for 2 hours.

Remove the slice from the tin, slice and serve.

Store remaining slices in an airtight container in the fridge for 1 week or in the freezer for up to 1 month.

Makes 16 large slices or 32 small slices

BASE

230 g (8 oz) raw cashew nuts

40 g (1½ oz) desiccated coconut

115 g (4 oz) soft medjool dates, pitted

1 teaspoon ground cinnamon

CARAMEL

40 g (1½ oz) tinned coconut cream

200 g (7 oz) soft medjool dates, pitted

150 g (5½ oz) hulled tahini

30 g (1 oz) coconut oil, melted

1 teaspoon vanilla extract

¼ teaspoon ground sea salt

CHOCOLATE

55 g (2 oz) cacao powder

100 g (3½ oz) coconut oil, melted

85 ml (2¾ fl oz) maple syrup

NOTE

You can also use 130 g (4½ oz) of vegan milk chocolate to melt on top instead of making your own.

STRAWBERRY BLONDE BARS

DAIRY FREE, GLUTEN FREE, VEGAN

Put the cashew nuts for the filling in a large bowl and cover with boiling water. Soak for 30 minutes.

Line the base and sides of a 20 cm × 20 cm × 7 cm deep (8 in × 8 in × 2¾ in) square springform cake tin with baking paper, allowing the sides to overhang. Set aside.

Blend the base ingredients and 30 ml (1 fl oz) water in your food processor until the mixture starts to come together. Press the mixture firmly into the base of your prepared tin. Freeze while you prepare the filling.

Drain and rinse the cashew nuts very well. Blend the cashew nuts, rice malt syrup, coconut oil, coconut cream, lemon juice and vanilla in your food processor until silky smooth and well combined.

Remove half the filling from the food processor and set aside. Add the strawberries to the food processor and blend until smooth. Pour the strawberry filling over the base and freeze for 1.5 hours.

Once set, pour the remaining filling over the strawberry layer. Freeze for 1 hour.

Before serving, sit at room temperature for 30 minutes. Carefully remove from the cake tin and discard the baking paper.

Cut into bars using a warm, sharp knife. Garnish each bar with a drizzle of melted coconut butter and chopped macadamia nuts. Decorate with a halved strawberry to serve.

Store the remaining bars in an airtight container in the freezer for up to 1 month.

Makes 18 bars

BASE

80 g (2¾ oz) medjool dates, pitted

80 ml (2½ fl oz/⅓ cup) rice malt syrup

50 g (1¾ oz) unsweetened desiccated coconut

170 g (6 oz) raw macadamia nuts

170 g (6 oz) buckwheat kernels

FILLING

300 g (10½ oz) raw cashew nuts

180 ml (6 fl oz) rice malt syrup

60 g (2 oz) coconut oil

400 ml (13½ fl oz) tinned coconut cream

60 ml (2 fl oz/¼ cup) freshly squeezed lemon juice

1 teaspoon vanilla extract

180 g (6½ oz) fresh strawberries, hulled

GARNISH

100 g (3½ oz) coconut butter, melted

9 fresh strawberries, halved

20 g (¾ oz) macadamia nuts, chopped

NOTE
You can use maple syrup in place of rice malt syrup.

MUESLI SLICE

DAIRY FREE, GLUTEN FREE, VEGAN

Line the base and sides of a 20 cm × 20 cm × 7 cm deep (8 in × 8 in × 2¾ in) square springform cake tin with baking paper, allowing the sides to overhang. Set aside.

Blend all the base ingredients in a food processor until the dough starts to stick together.

Using the back of a spoon, firmly press the base mixture evenly into the prepared tin. Freeze for 30 minutes.

Combine the pepitas, pecans, macadamia nuts, sesame seeds, cranberries, apricots and figs in a bowl. Mix well.

In a small saucepan over a low heat, melt the maple syrup, tahini, coconut butter, coconut sugar and cinnamon until combined. Remove from the heat, add the vanilla and mix well. Pour over the nut mixture and, using a strong arm, mix well.

Spread over the base, creating an even layer. Freeze for 1 hour.

Cut into slices then dip each slice into the melted white chocolate and place on baking paper until set.

Serve and enjoy.

Store the remaining slices in an airtight container in the freezer for up to 1 month.

Makes 24 mini slices

BASE

30 ml (1 fl oz) orange juice

1 tablespoon orange zest

145 g (5 oz) desiccated coconut

130 g (4½ oz) raw buckwheat kernels

130 g (4½ oz) soft medjool dates, pitted

40 g (1½ oz) cashew nut butter

TOPPING

80 g (2¾ oz) pepitas (pumpkin seeds)

80 g (2¾ oz) pecan halves, roughly chopped

80 g (2¾ oz) macadamia nuts, roughly chopped

1 tablespoon sesame seeds

80 g (2¾ oz) dried cranberries

80 g (2¾ oz) dried apricots, roughly chopped

80 g (2¾ oz) dried figs, finely sliced

100 ml (3½ fl oz) maple syrup

120 g (4½ oz) hulled tahini

60 g (2 oz) coconut butter

20 g (¾ oz) coconut sugar

1 teaspoon ground cinnamon

1 teaspoon vanilla extract

80 g (2¾ oz) vegan white chocolate, melted

NOTE
You can use melted coconut butter in place of white chocolate.

CAKES AND CHEESECAKES

DOUBLE CHOCOLATE CUPCAKES

DAIRY FREE, GLUTEN FREE, NUT FREE, VEGAN

Preheat the oven to 175°C (155°C fan forced/350°F). Line a 12-hole standard muffin tin with silicone cupcake liners.

In a small bowl, thoroughly mix the chia seeds and 30 ml (1 fl oz) water. Set aside to become gelatinous.

Whisk sugar, flour, cacao powder, baking powder, bicarbonate of soda and salt in a large bowl to combine. Mix coconut cream, applesauce, vanilla extract, boiling water and chia mixture in a separate bowl. Add the wet ingredients to the dry and mix until just combined. Divide the mixture evenly into the prepared silicone liners until they are three-quarters full.

Bake for 30–40 minutes or until a skewer inserted in the centre of a cupcake comes out with a few moist crumbs attached.

Stand the cupcakes in the tin for 5 minutes before turning them out, top-side up, onto a wire rack to cool completely.

Once cool, cut a deep circle into the top of each cupcake using the bottom of a small piping tip. Reserve the cut-outs for a chef's snack.

To make the caramel, blend the dates and sea salt in a food processor until small pieces remain. Slowly add 60 ml (2 fl oz/¼ cup) water until a thick caramel has formed. Set aside 70 g of the caramel for icing (frosting). Use the remaining caramel to fill the hole in each cupcake.

For the icing (frosting), mix all the ingredients in a high-speed blender or food processor until smooth and thick. Transfer the icing to a large bowl, cover with plastic wrap and refrigerate for 30 minutes to set.

Prepare a large piping (icing) bag with a closed star tip. Fill the bag with icing and pipe onto the cupcakes.

Serve and enjoy! The remaining cupcakes can be stored **in an airtight container in the fridge for 1 week.**

Makes 12

CAKE

2 teaspoons chia seeds

110 g (4 oz) rapadura sugar

135 g (5 oz) gluten-free plain (all-purpose) flour

45 g (1½ oz) cacao powder

¾ teaspoon baking powder

¾ teaspoon bicarbonate of soda (baking soda)

½ teaspoon ground sea salt

90 ml (3 fl oz) coconut cream

80 g (2¾ oz) applesauce

3 teaspoons vanilla extract

125 ml (4 fl oz/½ cup) boiling water

CARAMEL

210 g (7½ oz) soft medjool dates, pitted and roughly chopped

¼ teaspoon ground sea salt

ICING / FROSTING

50 g (1¾ oz) rapadura sugar

210 g (7½ oz) orange sweet potato purée (see note)

50 g (1¾ oz) cacao powder

15 g (½ oz) arrowroot starch

1 teaspoon vanilla extract

70 g (2½ oz) reserved caramel

20 g (¾ oz) coconut butter, melted

NOTE
For the orange sweet potato purée, steam or boil peeled orange sweet potato until tender. Drain and mash until a thick purée forms.

CAPPUCCINO CAKES

DAIRY FREE, GLUTEN FREE, VEGAN

When you need a sweet little kicker, these are made with real coffee to give you a shot in the arm.

Preheat the oven to 175°C (155°C fan forced/350°F). Line a 12-hole standard muffin tin with silicone cupcake liners.

In a small bowl, thoroughly mix the chia seeds and 115 ml (4 fl oz) water. Set aside to become gelatinous.

Pour the boiling water over the coffee granules and mix well. Set aside to cool to room temperature.

In a large bowl whisk the flour, sugar, salt and bicarbonate of soda to combine.

In a separate bowl, whisk the melted coconut oil, vanilla extract, coconut cream, chia mixture and cooled coffee mixture to combine.

Add the wet ingredients to the dry and mix until just combined.

Divide the mixture evenly into the prepared silicone liners, filling each liner to the top.

Bake for 35–40 minutes or until a skewer inserted into the centre of a cupcake comes out clean. Stand the cupcakes in the tin for 5 minutes before turning them out, top-side up, onto a wire rack to cool completely.

Bake the remaining cupcake mixture (it should make two more cupcakes).

For the icing (frosting), mix all the ingredients except the white chocolate in a high-speed blender or food processor until the icing is smooth and thick. Transfer to a large bowl, cover with plastic wrap and put in the freezer for 30 minutes to set.

Ice each cupcake with a thick layer of icing and a sprinkle of grated white chocolate.

Serve and enjoy!

Store the remaining cupcakes in an airtight container in the fridge for 1 week.

Makes 14

CAKE

30 g (1 oz) chia seeds

130 ml (4½ fl oz) boiling water

15 g (½ oz) instant coffee granules

420 g (15 oz) gluten-free plain (all-purpose) flour

150 g (5½ oz) rapadura sugar

¾ teaspoon ground sea salt

1½ teaspoons bicarbonate of soda (baking soda)

80 ml (2½ fl oz/⅓ cup) coconut oil, melted

3 teaspoons vanilla extract

300 ml (10 fl oz) tinned coconut cream

ICING / FROSTING

400 g (14 oz) white sweet potato purée (see note)

20 ml (¾ fl oz) espresso

1 teaspoon vanilla extract

100 g (3½ oz) rapadura sugar

3 teaspoons arrowroot starch

60 g (2 oz) cashew nut butter

30 ml (1 fl oz) plant-based milk

50 g (1¾ oz) vegan white chocolate, grated, to garnish

NOTE

For the white sweet potato purée, steam or boil peeled sweet potato until tender. Drain and mash until a thick purée forms.

LEMON MERINGUE CUPCAKES

DAIRY FREE, GLUTEN FREE, NUT FREE, VEGAN

Preheat the oven to 170°C (150°C fan forced/340°F). Line a 12-hole standard muffin tin with silicone cupcake liners.

In a large bowl, sift the flour, baking powder, cornflour, sugar and sea salt together. In a separate bowl mix the rice milk, applesauce, vanilla extract, lemon juice and lemon zest. Add the wet mixture to the dry and fold through until just incorporated. Fill the cupcake liners until they are three-quarters full. Bake for 40–45 minutes or until a skewer inserted into a cupcake comes out clean. Stand for 5 minutes before turning out, top-side up, onto a wire rack to cool.

To make the lemon curd, combine all the lemon curd ingredients in a small saucepan over a medium–high heat. Whisk continuously for 5–7 minutes or until the mixture is smooth and thickened. Remove from the heat and allow it to cool completely.

Cut a deep hole in the top of each cooled cupcake with a small piping tip. Be careful not to cut through to the bottom of the cupcake. Fill each hole with lemon curd.

Drain the chickpeas and reserve 145 ml (5 fl oz) of chilled chickpea water (aquafaba) in a large glass or metal mixing bowl. You want the bowl to be completely clean and free of grease. You can use lemon juice to clean the bowl and rinse before use. Using an electric mixer with a whisk attachment, whisk the chickpea aquafaba and cream of tartar on medium speed until stiff peaks form. Continue mixing and add the sugar one tablespoon at a time until it's incorporated. Once all the sugar is added continue whisking for a further minute. Add the vanilla and whisk for another 30 seconds.

Spoon the meringue into a piping (icing) bag with a large star-shaped nozzle and pipe it onto the cupcakes. Place under a preheated grill (broiler) until lightly golden, or use a small blowtorch to brown them.

Serve immediately and enjoy!

Makes 12

CAKE

200 g (7 oz) gluten-free plain (all-purpose) flour

2 teaspoons baking powder

2 tablespoons cornflour (cornstarch)

150 g (5½ oz) rapadura sugar

½ teaspoon ground sea salt

250 ml (8½ fl oz/1 cup) rice milk, room temperature

80 g (2¾ oz) unsweetened apple-sauce

2 teaspoons vanilla extract

2 tablespoons lemon juice

1 teaspoon finely grated lemon zest

LEMON CURD

125 ml (4 fl oz/½ cup) lemon juice

1 teaspoon finely grated lemon zest

30 ml (1 fl oz) tinned coconut milk

1 tablespoon cornflour (cornstarch)

¼ teaspoon turmeric

60 ml (2 fl oz/¼ cup) maple syrup

MERINGUE

400 g (14 oz) tin salt-free chickpeas, chilled overnight

½ teaspoon cream of tartar

145 g (5 oz) caster (superfine) sugar

½ teaspoon vanilla extract

NOTE

You can substitute the caster sugar in the meringue with 145 g (5 oz) of rapadura sugar mixed with 1 teaspoon of arrowroot starch. It will still work; however, it will produce a flatter meringue and a less airy texture.

RED VELVET CAKE

DAIRY FREE, GLUTEN FREE, NUT FREE, VEGAN

Red velvet will always hold a special place in my heart. This was the flavour and inspiration for my wedding cake. My creation uses beetroot (beet) powder and raspberry purée, which add a rich natural food colouring.

Line the base and sides of two 20 cm wide × 7 cm deep (8 in × 2¾ in) round springform cake tins with baking paper. Preheat the oven to 180°C (160°C fan forced/350°F).

Mix the milk and apple cider vinegar in a small bowl. Set aside for 10 minutes.

In a large bowl, sift flour, sugar, cacao powder, baking powder, cream of tartar and salt.

To the milk mixture add the melted coconut oil, raspberry purée, apple-sauce, lemon juice, beetroot powder and vanilla. Mix well. Add the wet mixture to the dry and mix to combine.

Evenly distribute the batter into the prepared cake tins. Bake for 25–35 minutes or until a skewer inserted into the centre of the cakes comes out clean.

Let the cakes cool in the tins for 10 minutes before turning out onto a wire rack to cool completely.

For the icing (frosting), mix all the ingredients in a high-speed blender or food processor until the icing is smooth and thick.

Sandwich the two cakes together using a third of the icing between the layers. Smooth the remaining icing over the entire cake and garnish with fresh strawberries.

Slice and serve!

Can be stored in an airtight container in the fridge for up to 3 days or sliced, wrapped in plastic wrap and frozen for up to 1 month.

Serves 12

CAKE

180 ml (6 fl oz) plant-based milk

30 ml (1 fl oz) apple cider vinegar

400 g (14 oz) gluten-free plain (all-purpose) flour

280 g (10 oz) rapadura sugar

1 tablespoon cacao powder

2 teaspoons baking powder

1 teaspoon cream of tartar

1 teaspoon ground sea salt

100 g (3½ oz) coconut oil, melted

240 g (8½ oz) frozen raspberries, warmed and mashed to a purée

110 g (4 oz) unsweetened applesauce

40 ml (1¼ fl oz) lemon juice

40 g (1½ oz) beetroot (beet) powder (see notes)

1 tablespoon vanilla extract

100 g (3½ oz) fresh strawberries to garnish

ICING / FROSTING

130 g (5 oz) vegan white chocolate, melted

50 g (1¾ oz) coconut butter, melted

200 ml (7 fl oz) coconut cream

200 g (7 oz) dessicated coconut

1 tablespoon arrowroot starch

1 teaspoon vanilla extract

NOTE

You can substitute 100 g (3½ oz) raw beetroot purée for the beetroot powder. If you take this option, you will have to reduce the raspberry purée to 140 g (5 oz) instead of 240 g (8½ oz).

TRIPLE-CHOC MUDCAKE

DAIRY FREE, GLUTEN FREE, NUT FREE, VEGAN

Line the base and sides of two 20 cm wide × 7 cm deep (8 in × 3 in) round springform cake tins with baking paper. Preheat the oven to 150°C (130°C fan forced/300°F).

In a small bowl, thoroughly mix the chia seeds and 80 ml (2½ fl oz/⅓ cup) water and set aside to become gelatinous.

In a large saucepan over a medium–low heat, heat the coconut oil, sugar, sweet potato, chocolate and milk. Heat until all the ingredients are melted and incorporated. Remove from the heat and add the chia mixture and vanilla. Mix well and set aside to cool.

In a large bowl, sift flour, cacao powder, baking powder and salt. Add the cooled chocolate mix and stir well.

Divide the mixture between the two prepared cake tins. Bake for 75–90 minutes. When you insert a skewer into the centre of the cakes, it will emerge with crumbs attached. Roll the crumbs from the skewer on your fingertips — if it balls and feels tacky, the cakes are ready!

Let the cakes cool in the tins for 10 minutes before turning out onto a wire rack to cool completely.

For the frosting, mix all the ingredients in a high-speed blender or food processor until smooth and thick.

Once the cakes are cool, place one cake on a serving plate. Top with the frosting, creating a smooth even layer. Top with the other cake and lightly press to securely position the cake on the frosting.

For the chocolate topping, combine all the ingredients in a bowl until smooth. Drizzle the chocolate over the cake.

Put in the refrigerator for 1 hour to set. Before serving, sift cacao powder over the cake.

Serve and enjoy!

Can be stored in an airtight container in the fridge for up to 4 days or sliced, wrapped in cling wrap and frozen for up to 1 month.

Serves 12

CAKE

20 g (¾ oz) chia seeds

100 g (3½ oz) coconut oil

280 g (10 oz) rapadura sugar

150 g (5½ oz) orange sweet potato purée (see note)

200 g (7 oz) vegan milk chocolate

375 ml (12½ fl oz/1½ cups) plant-based milk

3 teaspoons vanilla extract

220 g (8 oz) gluten-free plain (all-purpose) flour

25 g (1 oz) cacao powder

1 teaspoon baking powder

½ teaspoon ground sea salt

extra cacao powder for serving

FROSTING FOR FILLING

50 g (1¾ oz) rapadura sugar

250 g (9 oz) orange sweet potato purée (see note)

30 g (1 oz/¼ cup) cacao powder

3 teaspoons arrowroot starch

1 teaspoon vanilla extract

70 ml (2¼ fl oz) maple syrup

60 g (2 oz) vegan milk chocolate, melted

CHOCOLATE TOPPING

20 g (¾ oz) cacao powder

20 ml (¾ fl oz) maple syrup

40 g (1½ oz) coconut oil, melted

½ teaspoon vanilla extract

NOTE
To make the sweet potato purées, steam or boil peeled sweet potato until tender. Drain and mash to a smooth purée.

CHAI-CARROT CAKE

DAIRY FREE, GLUTEN FREE, VEGAN

Line the base and sides of two 20 cm (8 in) round springform cake tins with baking paper. Preheat the oven to 180°C (160°C fan forced/350°F).

In a small bowl mix the chia seeds and 125 ml (4 fl oz/ ½ cup) water. Set aside until thick and gelatinous.

Infuse the chai tea bag in the boiling water for 10 minutes until strong. Discard the tea bag.

In a large bowl, sift flour, baking powder, bicarbonate of soda, cinnamon, nutmeg, cloves, ginger and sea salt together. Add the grated carrot, sultanas, pistachios, walnuts and coconut and mix thoroughly.

In a separate bowl, beat the chia seed mixture, apple purée, rapadura sugar, coconut milk, maple syrup, vanilla extract and chai tea with an electric mixer until combined. Add the wet mixture to the dry and stir until just combined. Evenly fill the prepared cake tins.

Bake for 1.5 hours or until a toothpick inserted into the centre of the cakes comes out clean. Stand the cakes in the tins for 5 minutes before turning out, top-side up, onto wire racks to cool.

For the icing (frosting), put the cashew nuts in a small bowl, cover with boiling water and soak for 30 minutes. Drain and rinse well. Transfer to a high-speed blender or food processor. Add the sugar, arrowroot powder, sweet potato purée, lemon rind, sea salt, vanilla, lemon juice and milk and blend until smooth. Transfer to a large bowl and refrigerate until ready to use.

For the crumble, add the walnuts, pistachios, rice malt syrup, coconut oil and cinnamon to a small frying pan over a medium–low heat. Toast until the crumble is golden, fragrant and sticky. Set aside to cool.

Sandwich the two cakes together with a thick layer of icing. Smooth the remaining icing over the entire cake. Garnish with the crumble. Slice and serve!

Can be stored in an airtight container in the fridge for up to 4 days or sliced, wrapped in plastic wrap and frozen for up to 1 month.

Serves 12

CAKE

30 g (1 oz) chia seeds
90 ml (3 fl oz) boiling water
1 chai tea bag
450 g (1 lb) gluten-free plain (all-purpose) flour
3 teaspoons baking powder
2 teaspoons baking soda
2 teaspoons ground cinnamon
½ teaspoon ground nutmeg
⅛ teaspoon ground cloves
¼ teaspoon ground ginger
½ teaspoon ground sea salt
160 g (5½ oz) grated carrot
90 g (3 oz) sultanas (golden raisins)
80 g (2¾ oz) pistachios, chopped
80 g (2¾ oz) walnuts, chopped
60 g (2 oz) desiccated coconut
230 g (8 oz) apple purée
110 g (4 oz) rapadura sugar
400 ml (13½ fl oz) tinned coconut milk
165 ml (5½ fl oz) maple syrup
2 teaspoons vanilla extract

ICING / FROSTING

180 g (6½ oz) raw cashew nuts
100 g (3½ oz) rapadura sugar
2 teaspoons arrowroot powder
220 g (8 oz) orange sweet potato purée
2 teaspoons finely grated lemon rind
¼ teaspoon ground sea salt
1 teaspoon vanilla extract
1 tablespoon lemon juice
1 tablespoon plant-based milk

CRUMBLE

50 g (1¾ oz) walnuts, chopped
40 g (1½ oz) pistachios, chopped
60 ml (2 fl oz/¼ cup) rice malt syrup
1 teaspoon coconut oil
1 teaspoon cinnamon

DAD'S FRUITCAKE

DAIRY FREE, GLUTEN FREE, VEGAN

Dad would always brag about his fruitcakes, even if they were store bought. We'd enjoy a sneaky slice together for morning or afternoon tea.

Preheat the oven to 180°C (160°C fan forced/350°F). Line the base and sides of a 20 cm (8 in) round springform cake tin with baking paper.

In a saucepan over a medium–low heat, combine milk, apple purée, sugar and coconut oil. Stir until melted and combined. Set aside to cool.

In a large mixing bowl sift flour, bicarbonate of soda, cinnamon, nutmeg, cloves and sea salt. Add dates, figs, raisins, cranberries, orange zest, apricots and walnuts and mix well.

Add the wet mixture to the dry and stir well.

Pour into the prepared cake tin. Sprinkle the flaked almonds on the top and gently push into the batter. Bake for 1 hour or until a skewer inserted in the centre of the cake comes out clean.

Remove from the oven and allow to cool completely in the tin on a wire rack. Once cooled, remove from the tin and cut into slices.

Serve and enjoy! This cake freezes well – tightly wrap slices of cake in plastic wrap and freeze for up to 1 month.

Serves 12

125 ml (4 fl oz/½ cup) plant-based milk

320 g (11½ oz) apple purée

135 g (5 oz) rapadura sugar

60 g (2 oz) coconut oil

390 g (14 oz) gluten-free plain (all-purpose) flour

2 teaspoons bicarbonate of soda (baking soda)

1 ½ teaspoons ground cinnamon

½ teaspoon ground nutmeg

¼ teaspoon ground cloves

½ teaspoon ground sea salt

125 g (4½ oz) dried dates, pitted and roughly chopped

125 g (4½ oz) dried figs, roughly chopped

125 g (4½ oz) raisins

80 g (2¾ oz) dried cranberries

1 tablespoon finely grated orange zest

125 g (4½ oz) dried apricots, chopped

125 g (4½ oz) walnuts, chopped

50 g (1¾ oz) flaked almonds

NOTE
You can replace the walnuts and flaked almonds with sunflower kernels or pepitas (pumpkin seeds) for a nut-free fruitcake.

ORANGE & PASSIONFRUIT CHEESECAKE

DAIRY FREE, GLUTEN FREE, VEGAN

Put the cashew nuts in a large bowl and cover with boiling water. Soak for at least 30 minutes.

Line the base and sides of a 20 cm × 20 cm × 7 cm deep (8 in × 8 in × 3 in) square springform cake tin with baking paper.

Put all the base ingredients in a food processor and blend until the mixture forms a dough and starts to stick together. Using a wet spoon, press the base mixture onto the bottom of the prepared cake tin. Freeze while you prepare the filling.

Drain and rinse the soaked cashew nuts very well. Strain the passionfruit pulp to remove seeds.

Blend the rinsed cashew nuts, passionfruit pulp and remaining filling ingredients (except the garnishes) in your food processor or high-speed blender until very smooth.

Pour the filling over the base and smooth the top. Put in the freezer for 2 hours.

To serve, remove from the freezer and sit at room temperature for 30 minutes. Using a warm, sharp knife, cut the cheesecake into 12 bars. Garnish with the orange slices and drizzle over fresh passionfruit pulp.

Store the remaining cheesecake in an airtight container in the freezer for up to 1 month.

Serves 12

BASE

200 g (7 oz) pepitas (pumpkin seeds)

200 g (7 oz) sunflower kernels

100 g (3½ oz) desiccated coconut

150 g (5½ oz) soft medjool dates, pitted

50 g (1¾ oz) dried apricots, roughly chopped

¼ teaspoon ground sea salt

2 teaspoons ground cinnamon

¼ teaspoon ground ginger

1 tablespoon finely grated lemon zest

30 ml (1 fl oz) freshly squeezed lemon juice

FILLING

150 g (5½ oz) raw cashew nuts

170 g (6 oz) tinned passionfruit pulp

1 tablespoon finely grated orange zest

1 teaspoon orange extract (optional)

25 g (1 oz) goji berry powder

100 ml (3½ fl oz) freshly squeezed orange juice

130 ml (4½ fl oz) tinned coconut cream

50 ml (1¾ fl oz) rice malt syrup

80 g (2¾ oz) coconut oil

1 blood orange, thinly sliced, to garnish

1 fresh passionfruit, to garnish

TURKISH DELIGHT CHEESECAKE

DAIRY FREE, GLUTEN FREE, VEGAN

Put the cashew nuts for the filling in a large bowl and cover with boiling water. Soak for at least 30 minutes.

Line the base and sides of a 20 cm wide × 7 cm deep (8 in × 3 in) round springform cake tin with baking paper.

For the base, blend the macadamia nuts, desiccated coconut, buckwheat kernels and cacao powder in a food processor and mix to a crumb-like texture. Add the rice malt syrup, 30 ml (1 fl oz) water and the salt and pulse until well combined. Using a wet spoon, press the mixture onto the bottom of the prepared cake tin. Freeze while you prepare the filling.

Drain and rinse the soaked cashew nuts very well. Blend the cashew nuts, rice malt syrup, lemon juice, coconut oil, coconut cream and vanilla in a food processor or high-speed blender until very smooth.

Divide the filling equally into two bowls. In one bowl add the cacao powder and mix until smooth. In the second bowl add the beetroot powder and rosewater extract and mix well.

Dollop small amounts of each mixture on top of the prepared base, alternating between the two colours. Tap the cake tin on the bench to smooth the top. Using a skewer, gently swirl the two fillings together to create a marble effect. Freeze for 3 hours.

Carefully remove the cheesecake from the tin, discard the baking paper and transfer to a serving plate.

For the chocolate, mix the rosewater, cacao powder, melted coconut oil and maple syrup until smooth. Drizzle over the edge of the cheesecake and quickly garnish the top with dried cranberries and chopped pistachios. Refrigerate for 15 minutes to allow the chocolate to set.

Remove from the freezer and sit at room temperature for 30 minutes before serving.

Store the remaining cheesecake in an airtight container in the freezer for up to 1 month.

Serves 12

BASE

100 g (3½ oz) raw macadamia nuts

50 g (1¾ oz) unsweetened desiccated coconut

200 g (7 oz) buckwheat kernels

40 g (1½ oz/⅓ cup) cacao powder

80 ml (2½ fl oz/⅓ cup) rice malt syrup

¼ teaspoon ground sea salt

FILLING

300 g (10½ oz) raw cashew nuts

200 ml (7 fl oz) rice malt syrup

60 ml (2 fl oz/¼ cup) freshly squeezed lemon juice

50 g (1¾ oz) coconut oil, softened

400 ml (13½ fl oz) tinned coconut cream

½ teaspoon vanilla extract

1 teaspoon cacao powder

2 teaspoons beetroot (beet) powder

2 teaspoons rosewater extract

50 g (1¾ oz) dried cranberries, to garnish

40 g (1½ oz) pistachios, chopped, to garnish

CHOCOLATE

1 teaspoon rosewater

40 g (1½ oz/⅓ cup) cacao powder

60 g (2 oz) coconut oil, melted

20 ml (¾ fl oz) maple syrup

PEANUT BUTTER CHEESECAKE

DAIRY FREE, GLUTEN FREE, VEGAN

Jeremy, this one's for you: a rich chocolate base topped with creamy peanut butter layer and finished with a crunchy chocolate top. A peanut butter lovers dream!

Put the cashew nuts for the filling in a large bowl and cover with boiling water. Soak for at least 30 minutes.

Line the base and sides of a 20 cm wide × 7 cm deep (8 in × 3 in) round springform cake tin with baking paper.

Blend the walnuts, buckwheat kernels, cacao powder, dates, vanilla and 20 ml (¾ fl oz) water in a food processor and blitz until you get the texture of crumbs that stick together when pressed. Using a wet spoon, press the mixture onto the bottom of the prepared cake tin and put in the freezer while you prepare the filling.

Drain and rinse the soaked cashew nuts very well. Blend the cashew nuts, maple syrup, pumpkin purée, peanut butter, coconut cream and vanilla in a food processor or high-speed blender until very smooth.

Pour the filling over the base and smooth the top evenly. Put in the freezer for 2 hours to set.

To create the peanut topping, mix the peanuts, chocolate, 20 ml (¾ fl oz) water and maple syrup in a medium saucepan over a low heat. Mix until golden, fragrant and the chocolate has dissolved. Remove from the heat and add the sea salt, mixing well.

Pour the topping on top of the cheesecake and gently spread to create an even layer. Return the cheesecake to the freezer for 2 hours.

Carefully remove the cheesecake from the tin, discard the baking paper and transfer to a serving plate.

Allow the cheesecake to stand at room temperature for 30 minutes. Slice and enjoy!

Store the remaining cheesecake in an airtight container in the freezer for up to 1 month.

Serves 12

BASE

200 g (7 oz) raw walnuts

100 g (3½ oz) raw buckwheat kernels

40 g (1½ oz/⅓ cup) cacao powder

120 g (4½ oz) soft medjool dates, pitted

1 teaspoon vanilla extract

FILLING

300 g (10½ oz) raw cashew nuts

150 ml (5 fl oz) maple syrup

165 g (6 oz) pumpkin (squash) purée (see note)

170 g (6 oz) natural smooth peanut butter

200 ml (7 fl oz) coconut cream

1 teaspoon vanilla extract

PEANUT TOPPING

120 g (4½ oz/¾ cup) crushed peanuts

20 g (¾ oz) vegan milk chocolate, roughly chopped

30 ml (1 fl oz) maple syrup

¼ teaspoon ground sea salt

NOTE
To make the pumpkin purée, simply steam or boil the pumpkin until tender. Drain and mash to a smooth purée.

PUDDINGS
AND TARTS

PUMPKIN PECAN TART

DAIRY FREE, GLUTEN FREE, VEGAN

Pulse the sunflower kernels and almonds in a food processor until finely chopped. Add the flour, psyllium husk powder, ground cinnamon, cold coconut oil and coconut sugar. Process until the mixture resembles fine breadcrumbs.

Add the coconut yoghurt and vanilla. Process until the mixture starts to come together to form a smooth dough. Turn the mixture out onto a large piece of plastic wrap, shape into a disc and cover with plastic wrap. Refrigerate for 1 hour to rest.

In a small bowl, thoroughly mix the chia seeds and 30 ml (1 fl oz) of water. Set aside to become gelatinous.

In a clean food processor, blend the pumpkin purée, chia mixture, dates, vanilla extract, salt, cinnamon, ginger, nutmeg, coconut oil and 125 ml (4 fl oz/½ cup) water until a thick purée forms. Transfer to a large bowl and fold in three-quarters of the chopped pecans. Set aside.

Preheat the oven to 180°C (160°C fan forced/350°F).

Lightly brush a shallow 20 cm (8 in) round loose-base fluted flan (tart) tin with coconut oil. Evenly press the base into the tart tin, covering the bottom and sides.

Fill the pastry case with the filling. Smooth the surface and garnish with the remaining chopped pecans. Bake for 45 minutes or until the tart is golden and set.

Remove from the oven and set aside to cool for 30 minutes. Refrigerate for 2 hours to further set.

Best served with a dollop of coconut yoghurt.

Will keep in the fridge for up to 3 days.

Serves 8

BASE

20 g (¾ oz) raw sunflower kernels

30 g (1 oz) raw almonds

100 g (3½ oz) gluten-free plain (all-purpose) flour

¼ teaspoon psyllium husk powder

½ teaspoon ground cinnamon

65 g (2¼ oz) coconut oil, solid

30 g (1 oz) coconut sugar

40 g (1 ½ oz) coconut yoghurt

½ teaspoon vanilla extract

FILLING

2 teaspoons chia seeds

50 g (1¾ oz) pumpkin purée (see note)

150 g (5½ oz) soft medjool dates, pitted

1 teaspoon vanilla extract

¼ teaspoon ground sea salt

1 teaspoon ground cinnamon

¼ teaspoon ground ginger

¼ teaspoon ground nutmeg

20 g (¾ oz) coconut oil, softened

165 g (6 oz/1⅓ cups) pecans, roughly chopped

NOTE

To make the pumpkin purée, simply steam or boil peeled pumpkin until tender. Drain and mash to a smooth purée.

COCONUT LIME TART

DAIRY FREE, GLUTEN FREE, VEGAN

Grease a 3 cm (1 in) deep 28.5 cm × 18 cm (11¼ in × 7 in) loose-based rectangular flan (tart) tin with coconut oil.

Blend all the base ingredients and 30 ml (1 fl oz) water in a high-speed blender or food processor until the dough starts to stick together.

Using the back of a spoon, firmly press the base mixture evenly into the prepared tin, spreading evenly along the base and sides of the tin to form a shell. Freeze for 30 minutes.

Blend all the filling ingredients except the garnishes in a high-speed blender or food processor until smooth and creamy.

Pour this filling over the crust and smooth with a spatula. Freeze for 3 hours.

Once set, gently remove your tart from the tin and transfer to a serving plate. Garnish with the flaked coconut and lime zest.

Allow the tart to stand at room temperature for 15 minutes before slicing and enjoying!

Store in an airtight container in the freezer for up to 1 week.

Serves 8

BASE

80 g (2¾ oz) soft medjool dates, pitted

125 g (4½ oz) raw macadamia nuts

40 g (1½ oz) unsweetened desiccated coconut

75 g (2¾ oz) pepitas (pumpkin seeds)

FILLING

210 g (7½ oz) fresh avocado

90 ml (3 fl oz) freshly squeezed lime juice

1 tablespoon finely grated lime zest

160 g (5½ oz) coconut butter, softened

140 g (5 oz) tinned coconut cream

90 ml (3 fl oz) rice malt syrup

coconut flakes, to garnish

lime zest, to garnish

MINI CARAMEL TARTS

DAIRY FREE, GLUTEN FREE, VEGAN

Pulse the sunflower kernels and almonds in a food processor until finely chopped. Add the flour, psyllium husk powder, cinnamon, cold coconut oil and coconut sugar. Process until the mixture resembles fine breadcrumbs.

Add the vanilla and coconut yoghurt. Process until the mixture starts to come together to form a smooth dough. Turn the mixture out onto a large piece of plastic wrap, shape into a disc and cover with plastic wrap. Refrigerate for 1 hour to rest.

For the caramel, mix the coconut sugar, coconut cream, coconut oil, cornflour, milk and salt in a medium saucepan over a low heat. Whisk until the sugar has dissolved. Bring the mixture to a simmer and cook for 10–15 minutes, stirring frequently, until thickened.

Remove from the heat, then add the vanilla, mixing well. Set aside to cool for 15 minutes.

Preheat the oven to 180°C (160°C fan forced/350°F).

Lightly brush a 12-hole standard muffin tin with coconut oil.

Divide the dough into 12 equal portions, then evenly press into the muffin holes, covering the base and sides.

Fill each tart base with two teaspoons of the caramel and smooth the surface. Bake for 20–30 minutes or until the tart cases are golden and set.

Remove from the oven and set aside to cool in the tin for 30 minutes. Drizzle each tart with melted chocolate and refrigerate for 2 hours.

Remove from the muffin tin and serve.

Will keep in an airtight container in the fridge for up to 3 days.

Makes 12 mini tarts

BASE

40 g (1½ oz) raw sunflower kernels

60 g (2 oz) raw almonds

200 g (7 oz) gluten-free plain (all-purpose) flour

½ teaspoon psyllium husk powder

1 teaspoon ground cinnamon

125 g (4½ oz) coconut oil, solid

55 g (2 oz) coconut sugar

½ teaspoon vanilla extract

85 g (3 oz) coconut yoghurt

CARAMEL

240 g (8½ oz) coconut sugar

520 g (1 lb 2 oz) tinned coconut cream

60 g (2 oz) coconut oil

1 tablespoon cornflour (cornstarch)

30 ml (1 fl oz) plant-based milk

1 teaspoon ground sea salt

2 teaspoons vanilla extract

TOPPING

80 g (2¾ oz) vegan milk chocolate, melted

NOTES

You can replace the cornflour with arrowroot starch if you're avoiding corn.

You can also replace the coconut yoghurt in this recipe with Greek yoghurt if dairy isn't your enemy.

STICKY DATE DONUTS

DAIRY FREE, GLUTEN FREE, NUT FREE, VEGAN

Preheat the oven to 190°C (170°C fan forced/375°F). Lightly grease two 12-hole donut trays with melted coconut oil. Set aside.

In a small bowl thoroughly mix the chia seeds and 60 ml (2 fl oz/¼ cup) water. Set aside to become gelatinous.

Add the dates and bicarbonate of soda to a large bowl. Pour over boiling water and stir well. Set aside for 10 minutes to soften. Use a fork to mash the dates loosely, being sure to leave some chunks of goodness.

Sift the flour, baking powder and cinnamon together. Set aside.

Beat the coconut cream, vanilla and sugar together with an electric mixer until creamy. Add the chia mixture and beat until combined.

Fold in the date mixture with a spatula. Gently fold in the flour mixture.

Evenly fill 18 donut moulds to two-thirds full. Bake for 30 minutes or until a skewer inserted into a donut comes out clean.

To make the sauce, put the coconut oil, coconut sugar, coconut cream, cornflour and sea salt in a small saucepan over a low heat, stirring frequently to dissolve the sugar. Bring the mixture to a simmer and cook for 5 minutes, stirring frequently, until thickened slightly. Remove from the heat and add the vanilla, mixing well. Set aside to cool for 10 minutes.

To serve, remove the donuts from the trays. Drizzle the sauce over the top and add a sprinkle of dried dates.

Serve and enjoy.

Makes 18 donuts

DONUTS

25 g (1 oz) chia seeds

180 g (6½ oz) dried dates, pitted and roughly chopped

½ teaspoon bicarbonate of soda (baking soda)

300 ml (10 fl oz) boiling water

150 g (5½ oz) gluten-free plain (all-purpose) flour

1¼ teaspoon baking powder

1 teaspoon ground cinnamon

60 g (2 oz) tinned coconut cream

1 teaspoon vanilla extract

175 g (6 oz) coconut sugar

SAUCE

30 g (1 oz) coconut oil

120 g (4½ oz) coconut sugar

260 g (9 oz) tinned coconut cream

2 teaspoons cornflour (cornstarch)

½ teaspoon ground sea salt

1 teaspoon vanilla extract

TOPPING

60 g (2 oz) dried dates, pitted and roughly chopped

NOTE
You can substitute arrowroot starch for the cornflour.

MANGO, TURMERIC & GINGER PUDDING

DAIRY FREE, GLUTEN FREE, VEGAN

Mix the frozen mango, ginger, turmeric, milk, dates, cashew nut butter and vanilla in a high-speed blender until smooth.

Transfer to an airtight container and add the chia seeds. Mix well. Cover and refrigerate overnight to set.

The next day, spoon the pudding into serving bowls and top with chopped pistachios and fresh raspberries. Enjoy!

Serves 2

150 g (5½ oz) frozen mango
½ teaspoon ground ginger
¼ teaspoon ground turmeric
300 ml (10 fl oz) plant-based milk
50 g (1¾ oz) medjool dates, pitted
30 g (1 oz) cashew nut butter
1 teaspoon vanilla extract
60 g (2 oz) chia seeds
pistachios, chopped, to serve
fresh raspberries, to serve

CHOCOLATE PUDDING

DAIRY FREE, GLUTEN FREE, VEGAN

Don't fear the avocado! After this pudding has had time to rest you won't even notice it's hiding in there!

Mix all the ingredients (except the garnishes) in a high-speed blender or food processor until completely smooth.

Transfer to a small bowl and refrigerate for at least 3 hours.

Scoop into bowls and garnish with the crushed nuts and fresh strawberries, or toppings of your choice!

Serves 2

100 g (3½ oz) ripe avocado
1 teaspoon vanilla extract
25 g (1 oz) cacao powder
120 g (4½ oz) soft medjool dates, pitted
crushed peanuts, to serve
fresh strawberries, to serve

NOTE
You can add a tablespoon of almond butter if you want an extra-creamy pudding.

JAFFA PUDDING

DAIRY FREE, GLUTEN FREE, NUT FREE, VEGAN

I used to love Jaffas, so I've reinvented the classic treat in this gooey pudding. Best served fresh and hot.

Preheat the oven to 190°C (170°C fan forced/375°F). Lightly grease a 20.8 cm × 8.6 cm deep (8 in × 3¼ in) ring (bundt) tin with coconut oil. Set aside.

In a small bowl thoroughly mix the chia seeds and 60 ml (2 fl oz/¼ cup) water. Set aside to become gelatinous.

Put the dates and bicarbonate of soda in a large bowl. Pour over the boiling water and orange juice and stir well. Set aside for 10 minutes to soften. Transfer to a high-speed blender and mix until it becomes a smooth purée.

Sift the flour, baking powder and cacao powder together. Set aside.

Beat the coconut cream, vanilla and sugar together with an electric mixer until creamy. Add the chia mixture and orange zest and beat until combined. Add the date purée and beat well. Gently fold in the flour mixture with a spatula.

Pour into the prepared tin. Bake for 60–75 minutes or until a skewer inserted into the centre of the pudding comes out with a few moist crumbs attached.

Cool in the tin for 5 minutes before removing and transferring to a serving plate.

To make the sauce, stir the coconut oil, rice malt syrup, coconut cream, orange juice, orange zest and cornflour in a small saucepan over a low heat. Stir well and bring the mixture to a simmer. Cook for 5 minutes, stirring frequently until thickened.

Remove from the heat. Add the vanilla and goji powder and mix well. Set aside to cool for 10 minutes.

Pour the sauce over the warm pudding and garnish with fine orange zest.

Store the remaining pudding in an airtight container in the fridge for up to 3 days.

Serves 6

PUDDING

25 g (1 oz) chia seeds

180 g (6½ oz) dried dates, pitted and roughly chopped

½ teaspoon bicarbonate of soda (baking soda)

250 ml (8½ fl oz/1 cup) boiling water

100 ml (3½ fl oz) orange juice

150 g (5½ oz) gluten-free plain (all-purpose) flour

1¼ teaspoon baking powder

30 g (1 oz/¼ cup) cacao powder

60 g (2 oz) tinned coconut cream

1 teaspoon vanilla extract

175 g (6 oz) coconut sugar

1 tablespoon finely grated orange zest

SAUCE

3 teaspoons coconut oil

25 ml (¾ fl oz) rice malt syrup

75 g (2¾ oz) tinned coconut cream

40 ml (1¼ fl oz) freshly squeezed orange juice

1 tablespoon finely grated orange zest

1 teaspoon cornflour (cornstarch)

½ teaspoon vanilla extract

1 teaspoon goji berry powder

TOPPING

1 tablespoon fine orange zest

NOTE
You can substitute arrowroot flour for the cornflour.

133

APPLE & APRICOT CRUMBLE

DAIRY FREE, GLUTEN FREE, VEGAN

Preheat the oven to 180°C (160°C fan forced/350°F).

Cut the apple into 2 cm (¾ in) dice and put in a large bowl. Add the remaining filling ingredients and mix to combine. Transfer to a 1.5 litre (51 fl oz/6 cup) capacity ovenproof dish.

Pulse the walnuts in a food processor until they form a flour. Add the remaining crumble ingredients and pulse until a dough forms.

Tip the mixture out onto a floured bench and bring together with your hands to form a flat disc. Wrap in plastic wrap and freeze for 30 minutes.

Once chilled, crumble the dough evenly over the apple mixture. Top with chopped pistachios.

Bake for 40–50 minutes or until golden and the apple is cooked. Serve hot or warm. Delicious with Chai ice cream (page 144).

Serves 6

FILLING

400 g (14 oz) raw green apples

40 ml (1¼ fl oz) freshly squeezed orange juice

100 g (3½ oz) sultanas (golden raisins)

160 g (5½ oz) dried apricots, roughly chopped

60 g (2 oz) rapadura sugar

1 teaspoon vanilla extract

1 teaspoon ground cinnamon

½ teaspoon arrowroot starch

CRUMBLE

75 g (2¾ oz) raw walnuts

200 g (7 oz) gluten-free oat flour

¾ teaspoon psyllium husk

55 g (2 oz) rapadura sugar

80 g (2¾ oz) coconut oil

125 g (4½ oz/½ cup) tinned coconut cream

1 teaspoon apple cider vinegar

¼ teaspoon ground nutmeg

¼ teaspoon ground ginger

TOPPING

30 g (1 oz) raw pistachio nuts, chopped

NOTE
Feel free to use any fruit you like!
Pears or peaches would also work well.

STREET
TREATS

DONUTS

DAIRY FREE, GLUTEN FREE, VEGAN

Preheat the oven to 180°C (160°C fan forced/350°F).

Grease a 12-hole donut tin with coconut oil. Set aside.

Drain the chickpeas, reserving 120 ml (4½ fl oz) of the liquid (aquafaba). Transfer the chickpeas to a sealed container in the fridge and keep for another use. Whisk the chickpea aquafaba until frothy.

Add the dry ingredients to a large bowl and whisk to combine. Make a well in the centre and add the frothy aquafaba, apple cider vinegar, vanilla extract and milk. Mix until just combined.

Spoon the batter evenly into the prepared donut tin, filling the moulds three-quarters of the way up. Bake for 10 minutes or until lightly golden and puffed. Cool in the tin for 5 minutes then remove to a cooling rack.

Dip some donuts into the melted chocolate and return to the cooling rack to set. Dip other donuts into the melted coconut butter and return to the cooling rack to set. Drizzle donuts with peanut butter, freeze-dried strawberries, coconut flakes and crushed peanuts. Get creative and decorate!

Serve and enjoy! Donuts are best eaten fresh.

Makes 12 small donuts

DONUTS

400 g (14 oz) tin salt-free chickpeas

165 g (6 oz) gluten-free plain (all-purpose) flour

65 g (2¼ oz) rapadura sugar

¼ teaspoon ground nutmeg

1 teaspoon baking powder

1 teaspoon bicarbonate of soda (baking soda)

1 teaspoon apple cider vinegar

1 teaspoon vanilla extract

125 ml (4 fl oz/½ cup) plant-based milk

TOPPING

100 g (3½ oz) vegan milk chocolate, melted

150 g (5½ oz) coconut butter, melted

35 g (1¼ oz) smooth peanut butter

30 g (1 oz) coconut flakes

30 g (1 oz) freeze-dried strawberries, crushed

30 g (1 oz) crushed peanuts

NUTTER BUTTER CUPS

DAIRY FREE, GLUTEN FREE, VEGAN

Line a 12-hole standard muffin tin with nine silicone liners.

Mix half the cacao powder, half the maple syrup and half the melted coconut oil together until smooth.

With a small spoon, evenly distribute the chocolate mixture into the silicone liners. Lightly drop the muffin tin on the bench a few times to flatten the chocolate. Freeze for 15 minutes.

In a small saucepan add the peanut butter, coconut sugar and condensed milk. Mix over a low heat until the sugar has dissolved. Drop a spoonful of the peanut mixture over the chilled chocolate layer, in each of the silicone liners, and spread to create an even layer. Freeze for 15 minutes.

Mix the remaining cacao powder, maple syrup and coconut oil together. Spoon over the peanut layer and tap the tray on the bench again to flatten the last layer. Freeze for a further 15 minutes.

Remove each cup from its silicone liner and serve!

Store the remaining cups in the freezer for up to 1 month.

Makes 9

CHOCOLATE

100 g (3½ oz) cacao powder

100 ml (3½ fl oz) maple syrup

120 g (4½ oz) coconut oil, melted

PEANUT LAYER

140 g (5 oz) smooth peanut butter

50 g (1¾ oz) coconut sugar

100 g (3½ oz) coconut condensed milk

NOTE
Feel free to use any filling you like! Try a seed butter if you are avoiding nuts.

PANCAKES

DAIRY FREE, GLUTEN FREE, NUT FREE, VEGAN

Combine all the ingredients in a blender until smooth. Set batter aside for 10 minutes to thicken.

Heat a non-stick pan over a medium heat and lightly coat with coconut oil.

Drop spoonfuls of batter onto the pan and wait until bubbles form before flipping each pancake. Cook until golden on both sides.

Serve with Chocolate hazel nut butter, pure maple syrup or your choice of toppings.

FLAVOUR COMBINATIONS

Blueberry: Stir some blueberries into the pancake batter for a burst of sweetness.

Carrot cake: Stir 1 teaspoon of cinnamon and 1 table-spoon of sultanas into the batter with ¼ cup grated carrot before cooking.

Red velvet: Stir 1 teaspoon of beetroot (beet) powder into the batter and top the finished pancakes with coconut yoghurt and shredded coconut.

Makes 10 small pancakes

90 g (3 oz) gluten-free rolled oats

150 g (5½ oz) gluten-free plain (all-purpose) flour

1 teaspoon psyllium husk

1 tablespoon baking powder

2 teaspoons vanilla extract

350 ml (6 fl oz) plant-based milk

2 medjool dates (approx. 40 g/1½ oz), pitted

150 g (5½ oz) apple purée

NOTE
You can substitute solidified coconut cream for the apple purée if needed.

143

CHOCOLATE HAZEL NUT BUTTER

DAIRY FREE, GLUTEN FREE, VEGAN

In a food processor or high-powered blender, blend the hazelnuts and process until they have a creamy butter consistency. Occasionally scrape down the sides of the bowl – and have patience — it will eventually turn to butter. Add the remaining ingredients and blend until silky smooth.

Serve on top of pancakes, a dollop in smoothies, smeared on toast — the sky is the limit!

Store nut butter in the fridge for up to 1 month.

250 g (9 oz) dry-roasted hazelnuts

25 g (1 oz) cacao powder

25 ml (¾ fl oz) vanilla extract

¼ teaspoon ground sea salt

120 ml (4 fl oz) plant-based milk

130 g (4½ oz) soft medjool dates, pitted

ICE CREAM

DAIRY FREE, GLUTEN FREE, NUT FREE, VEGAN

Line a loaf (bar) tin or 1-litre (34 fl oz/4 cup) ice cream tub with baking paper.

Using an electric mixer, whisk together all of the ice cream ingredients for 15 minutes or until soft peaks form. You want the consistency of whipped cream.

Add desired flavours (see below) and whisk to combine.

Transfer the mixture to the prepared container. Cover with a lid or plastic wrap and foil. Freeze overnight.

Remove the ice cream from the freezer 20 minutes prior to scooping. Enjoy!

Makes approximately 1 litre (34 fl oz/4 cups)

200 g (7 oz) coconut condensed milk

600 ml (20½ fl oz) tinned coconut cream

1 teaspoon vanilla extract

NOTES

Get creative with flavours and try your own combinations.

This ice cream is best served soon after initial freezing time, as it tends to go solid after a few days.

ICE CREAM FLAVOURS

CHAI

1 teaspoon cinnamon
¼ teaspoon ginger
¼ teaspoon nutmeg

PEPPERMINT

½ teaspoon peppermint extract
¼ teaspoon spirulina
¼ teaspoon vegan green food colouring
½ teaspoon cacao powder

COOKIE DOUGH

4 crumbled Cookie dough treats (page 61)

ESPRESSO

2 teaspoons ground espresso
20 g (¾ oz) cacao powder

STRAWBERRY

100 g (3½ oz) puréed strawberries
50 g (1¾ oz) vegan white chocolate chips

RUM & RAISIN

150 g (5½ oz) raisins
50 ml (1¾ fl oz) dark sweet rum

Put raisins and rum in a saucepan over a medium heat and bring to the boil. Remove from the heat and allow to cool. Fold through the ice cream base mixture.

SALTED CARAMEL

130 g (4½ oz) soft medjool dates, pitted
½ teaspoon ground sea salt

Blend dates in a food processor with salt until a purée forms, adding water if needed. Stir the purée through the ice cream base mixture.

CHURROS

DAIRY FREE, GLUTEN FREE, NUT FREE, VEGAN

For the dipping sauce, mix the coconut sugar, coconut cream and sea salt in a small saucepan over a low heat, frequently stirring to dissolve the sugar. Bring the mixture to a simmer and cook for 5 minutes. Remove from the heat and add the vanilla, mixing well. Set aside to cool.

For the churros, preheat the oven to 200°C (180°C fan forced/400°F). Line a large 38 cm × 25 cm (15 in × 10 in) baking tray (cookie sheet) with baking paper.

In a medium saucepan over a low heat stir 250 ml (8½ fl oz/1 cup) water, 30 g (1¼ oz) of the sugar and the salt until they have dissolved. Remove from the heat and add the coconut oil and vanilla, mixing well. Add the flour and psyllium husk and stir until combined.

Transfer the mixture to a piping (icing) bag with a large star tip. Pipe long strips of dough onto your prepared baking tray, leaving a 3 cm (1 in) space between each churro. You can pipe the churros to be as long as you like — get creative!

Bake for 15–20 minutes or until the churros are nicely puffed and golden.

Combine the remaining sugar and ground cinnamon in a sealable bag and shake to combine. Put the churros one by one inside the bag and shake to evenly coat. Serve immediately alongside the caramel dipping sauce and melted chocolate.

Makes 12 large churros

CARAMEL DIPPING SAUCE

30 g (1 oz) coconut sugar

65 g (2¼ oz) tinned coconut cream

¼ teaspoon ground sea salt

¼ teaspoon vanilla extract

CHURROS

60 g (2 oz) rapadura sugar

½ teaspoon ground sea salt

30 g (1 oz) coconut oil

1 teaspoon vanilla extract

215 g (7½ oz) gluten-free plain (all-purpose) flour

1 teaspoon psyllium husk

1 teaspoon ground cinnamon

70 g (2½ oz) coconut milk chocolate, melted, to serve

NOTE
Feel free to use any dipping sauce you like!

CHOCOLATE CHIP COOKIES

DAIRY FREE, GLUTEN FREE, NUT FREE, VEGAN

In a small bowl, thoroughly mix the chia seeds and 20 ml (¾ fl oz) water. Set aside to become gelatinous.

In a bowl, beat the coconut oil and sugar with an electric mixer for 3–4 minutes until creamy and combined. Add the chia mixture and vanilla, and beat until well combined.

In a large bowl, sift flour, baking powder and bicarbonate of soda. Add the wet ingredients and mix with a spatula until combined. Gently fold through the chocolate chunks and sea salt. Refrigerate the dough for 20 minutes.

Preheat the oven to 180°C (160°C fan forced/350°F). Line two 38 cm × 25 cm (15 in × 10 in) baking trays (cookie sheets) with baking paper.

Using wet hands, scoop a tablespoon of the mixture, roll it into a ball and place on the baking tray. Repeat with the remaining mixture. Be sure to leave plenty of room between each cookie as the dough will spread!

Bake for 10–12 minutes.

Remove from the oven and cool on a wire rack before eating.

Store remaining cookies in the fridge for up to 4 days.

Makes 16

1 teaspoon chia seeds

80 g (2¾ oz) coconut oil

155 g (5½ oz) rapadura sugar

1 teaspoon vanilla extract

150 g (5½ oz) gluten-free plain (all-purpose) flour

½ teaspoon baking powder

¼ teaspoon bicarbonate of soda (baking soda)

60 g (2 oz) vegan chocolate, cut into 2 cm (¾ in) chunks

¼ teaspoon ground sea salt

SALTED CARAMEL COOKIES FOR TWO

DAIRY FREE, GLUTEN FREE, NUT FREE, VEGAN

Soft-centred jumbo cookies for those lazy nights when you need a quick and easy treat. Perfectly paired with a cup of tea, one for me and one for you.

Preheat the oven to 180°C (160°C fan forced/350°F). Line a 38 cm × 25 cm (15 in × 10 in) baking sheet (cookie sheet) with baking paper.

In a small bowl, thoroughly mix the chia seeds with 30 ml (1 fl oz) water. Set aside to become gelatinous.

Add all the remaining ingredients except the chocolate to a large bowl. Mix in the chia mixture until a wet dough forms. Fold in half the chopped chocolate.

Split the dough into two and shape into two large discs on the baking sheet. Stud the dough with remaining chocolate.

Bake for 20 minutes for a soft, gooey cookie.

Makes 2 jumbo cookies

1 tablespoon chia seeds

60 g (2 oz) tinned coconut cream

60 g (2 oz) coconut sugar

¼ teaspoon ground sea salt

½ teaspoon vanilla extract

100 g (3½ oz) brown rice flour

¼ teaspoon bicarbonate of soda (baking soda)

50 g (1¾ oz) dairy-free salted caramel chocolate, roughly chopped

Not a fan of salted caramel? No problem! Here are some other flavour combinations:

STICKY DATE

Replace the chocolate with 50 g (1¾ oz/¼ cup) chopped dates, ¼ cup chopped pecans and 1 teaspoon of cinnamon.

WHITE CHOCOLATE

Replace the caramel chocolate with 25 g (1 oz/¼ cup) of vegan white choc chips, 25 g (1 oz/¼ cup) dried cranberries and 25 g (1 oz/¼ cup) chopped macadamia nuts.

CHOC CHIP

Replace the caramel chocolate with vegan milk chocolate.

RAINBOW MERINGUE

DAIRY FREE, GLUTEN FREE, NUT FREE, VEGAN

Meringue with no eggs? The transformation of chickpea water (aquafaba) to fluffy meringue is genius. I've discovered caster sugar works best for this recipe — one of the only times I use refined sugar.

Preheat the oven to 100°C (80°C fan forced/200°F). Prepare a large clean glass or metal mixing bowl that's completely clean and free of grease.

Using an electric mixer, whisk the chickpea aquafaba and cream of tartar on medium speed until stiff peaks form. Continue mixing, adding the sugar one tablespoon at a time until all incorporated. Whisk for a further minute, add the vanilla and whisk briefly again.

Working quickly, divide the mixture into three separate clean bowls. To make three meringue colours, add a drop of food colouring to each bowl and gently fold through to make yellow, pink and blue meringue.

Prepare a piping (icing) bag with a large star-shaped nozzle. Spoon a dollop of yellow meringue into the piping (icing) bag, top with pink meringue and then blue. Repeat until all the meringue is used. Be gentle with the mixture so it doesn't deflate.

Line a large baking sheet (cookie sheet) with baking paper. Pipe small circles onto the baking paper. Be sure to only create one even layer so it bakes evenly.

Bake for 3.5 hours or until the meringues feel firm on the outside. Do not open the door to tap the meringues until at least 2 hours have passed.

Leave the cooked meringues in the oven to cool for 1.5–2 hours, which will allow the meringues to firm up inside. Do not open the oven door.

Once cool, remove the meringues from the oven and slide onto a serving platter. Serve with the mixed berries and yoghurt and nuts. Enjoy!

You can store the meringues in an airtight container in the fridge until ready to use.

Serves 12

MERINGUE

400 g (14 oz) tin salt-free chickpeas, chilled, strain and set aside 145 ml (5 fl oz) of the chickpea liquid (aquafaba)

½ teaspoon cream of tartar

145 g (5 oz) caster (superfine) sugar

½ teaspoon vanilla extract

vegan yellow food colouring

vegan pink food colouring

vegan blue food colouring

OPTIONAL GARNISHES

coconut yoghurt, to serve

fresh mixed berries, to serve

chopped hazelnuts (optional for nut free)

NOTE

You can substitute 145 g (5 oz) of rapadura sugar mixed with 1 teaspoon arrowroot starch for the caster sugar. It will still work; however, it will produce a flatter meringue and a less airy texture.

BREAKFAST SMOOTHIE

DAIRY FREE, GLUTEN FREE, VEGAN

Place all the smoothie ingredients in a high-speed blender and blend until smooth and thick.

Pour into two glasses and enjoy!

Serves 2

40 g (1½ oz) gluten-free rolled oats

400 ml (13½ fl oz) plant-based milk

100 g (3½ oz) frozen pear, cored

30 g (1 oz) almond butter

¼ teaspoon vanilla extract

NOTES

You can use any plant-based milk in this recipe. I love using coconut milk.

You can also use your favourite gluten-free granola or muesli instead of oats.

CHERRY CHOCOLATE SMOOTHIE

DAIRY FREE, GLUTEN FREE, NUT FREE, VEGAN

This tastes like a chocolate thickshake. You know, the one drink you feel naughty ordering from your local cafe. Now you can drink up and not feel one ounce of guilt. Thank me later.

Put all the ingredients in a high-speed blender and mix until thick and smooth.

Pour into two glasses and enjoy!

Serves 2

350 g (12½ oz) frozen cherries

40 g (1½ oz) fresh spinach leaves

65 g (2¼ oz) medjool dates, pitted

25 g (1 oz) cacao powder

¼ teaspoon vanilla extract

400 ml (13½ fl oz) coconut milk

20 g (¾ oz) chia seeds

NOTE

You can use any plant-based milk in this recipe. I love using coconut milk.

STRAWBERRIES & CREAM SMOOTHIE

DAIRY FREE, GLUTEN FREE, NUT FREE, VEGAN

Place oats, frozen strawberries, dates, vanilla and coconut milk in a high-speed blender. Mix until thick and smooth.

Using two mason jars, place a small amount of smoothie mixture in the bottom of each jar. Top with some of the coconut yoghurt and more smoothie mixture. Continue this process until you have used all the smoothie mixture and coconut yoghurt. Top smoothies with strawberries and flaked coconut. Serve with a spoon and enjoy!

Serves 2

50 g (1¾ oz) gluten-free oats
320 g (11½ oz) frozen strawberries
30 g (1 oz) soft medjool dates, pitted
¼ teaspoon vanilla extract
300 ml (10 fl oz) coconut milk
200 g (7 oz) coconut yoghurt
fresh strawberries to serve
flaked coconut to serve

NOTE
You can use any plant-based milk in this recipe. I love using coconut milk.

INDEX

A BIG THANK YOU
FROM THE HEART

In creating this book, I've been honoured to work with some of the most inspirational and talented people in my life today. Their guidance and creative influence have transformed my humble recipes into the beautiful book you're holding now.

First and foremost, a huge thank you to Jeremy. Not only are you my husband, but my forever soulmate, best friend, business partner and self-declared number one fan. With you, we've built this life I adore, created a community that I treasure and shaped the confidence to share my soul with the world. Your endless late nights designing creative food ideas and your brave taste testing never go unnoticed. I am the luckiest woman in the world to have you by my side. I love you with every inch of my being, and I thank you so much.

Pam Brewster, the wonderful woman who believed in me and connected with my vision. Thank you for bringing my dream to life and seeing potential in the little things. Your support means the world and *The Healthy Convert* would not be a reality without your honest and respectful guidance. Thank you for taking the time to touch my life in such a beautiful way.

Thankyou Allison Hiew and Marg Bowman. If I write from the heart, then you are my trusted eyes, voice, ears and mind. Your editing and attention to detail have saved this book many times over.

Michelle Mackintosh and Mark Campbell, my lovely, talented designers. Thank you for creating a book I will cherish for the rest of my life. You have both been an absolute joy to collaborate with and your kindness and never-ending patience will be remembered forever.

A special thanks to Elisa Watson, my incredible photographer, and Georgia Young, my superb food stylist. Your love of food and infinite knowledge were truly appreciated. You never failed to reach plate perfection and capture those precious moments. Thank you for all your hard work, I look forward to working with you both again in the future.

To all the lovely people at Hardie Grant, thank you for working with me. From the moment I met you, your approachability and caring nature warmed my heart. You're a dream to work with and I couldn't have picked a better team to collaborate with on my first book. Thank you for being a part of my journey and I am truly grateful for everything you do.

With great affection and gratitude I would like to thank my family and friends. You have all helped shape the person I am today with your endless support, love, understanding and honest taste testing. You encourage me to be the best version of myself and I love having you all by my side on this wondrous journey. I hope to shower you all with healthy sweet treats over the coming years.

Most importantly, a big warm thank you goes to you, my reader, for following my journey, connecting with me daily, supporting my blog and purchasing this book. I hope to continuously provide you with a spark of inspiration in the kitchen and motivation to try something new. I urge you to share this book with your friends. Treat these recipes as if they were your own. Brag about sweet potato icing to everyone you meet. Try something new and always remember to bring joy, love and soul to each plate, because beautiful food can create memories that last forever.

Nicole Maree x